FROM THE HEART

June Carter Cash.

June Carter Cash

FROM THE
HEART

PRENTICE HALL PRESS · NEW YORK

Published by Prentice Hall Press
A Division of Simon & Schuster, Inc.
Gulf + Western Building
One Gulf + Western Plaza
New York, N.Y. 10023

PRENTICE HALL PRESS is a trademark of Simon & Schuster, Inc.

Library of Congress Cataloging-in-Publication Data

Cash, June Carter, 1929–
 From the heart.

 1. Cash, June Carter, 1929–   . 2. Country
musicians—United States—Biography.   I. Title.
ML420.C2653A3   1987   784.5'2'00924 [B]   86-43149
ISBN: 0-13-530767-8

Designed by Patricia Fabricant

Manufactured in the United States of America

10 9 8 7 6 5 4 3 2 1

First Edition

Because I've had to pray sometimes for what seemed impossible, I find myself content with my life and my Lord. Heaven knows, I've sometimes had to pray a lot more than I had meant to. . . .

This book is for my "babies:" Carlene, Rosey, John Carter, Rose-anne, Kathy, Cindy, and Tara. For Waylon, Kris, Larry, and Joe, and of course for John, the biggest baby of them all.

Contents

Preface

I wanted to call this book *Out of My Mind* at one point—because some of the things you'll read about here tell about my hurt, confusion, and despair with life. As I searched deeper into my mind, I also gleaned the joy—the wonderful "soaring" of the heart—as I lived my life. God did hear my prayers, and if reading this book will show you how to strengthen your faith and learn to live thanking God for all things good and bad, then I've chosen to share some of my innermost secrets and thoughts with you. Steel is strong because of the hammer and the fire.

I do believe God sat me beside my editor, Bill Thompson, on an airplane, and from our conversation, and later through my friend Katy Edelman, he asked me to write a book. I remember telling him "I don't have anything to say." This was at a time when John was in the Betty Ford Center and I was low, low, low.

I sat down two years later and started to write of random things that had special meaning to me. It wasn't hard for me—after all I had lived it and it had been intense. My highs and lows are here with my tears and laughter and I want you here with me.

When things seemed impossible, I got down on my knees and prayed. I covered my head with my arms, lay prostrate on the floor, and waited while God poured out his blessings on me.

I face today, giving God the credit for reminding me how much I love my husband, my family, and my friends—I could have lost you all.

Be a new friend of mine, if you can.

My love and prayers,
June Carter Cash

COME BACK TO JAMAICA

Our Jamaican house is called Cinnamon Hill, and we'd go there when we wanted to stop time and put our feet up and have a family vacation! The island is warm, beautiful, and peaceful, but maybe there's no such place.

Cinnamon Hill Great House. Montego Bay, Jamaica.

Don't run, John Jackson." I screamed. "Walk." But then why shouldn't he run? We were all running as fast as we could. We were responding to the cry of death. The high-pitched scream of a thirty-year-old Jamaican woman. You just knew it. The breeze—or was it a breeze—was thick with the smell of blood. I felt as if it had not only flowed over my senses but was bathing me in the horror of it all. A living nightmare in which I was the star. We moved in slow motion—four security guards running with ease, their guns drawn. But they seemed to be moving about five feet above the ground as a duppie would—going, but not in a hurry.

The time 1986; but the scene could have been somewhere back in time, for the Great House remained the same. Tall, stone, proud, harsh, strong as the ancestors that had built it in 1741; The Cinnamon Hill Great House breathed the dignity of the Barretts of Wimpole Street. But the hurt and agony of ghosts of the slave trade resounded again and again in the voice of that thirty-year-old woman, crying "God help us, somebody up there help us, Lord."

Karen, our young Jamaican maid, cried, "Don't look, Ma'am." But I wanted to look. I wanted to see—I wanted to hear the sound of death—or smell it. I wanted to know it all. My grandson, John Jackson, wanted to see also. I could read his thoughts: "Just like TV, grandma. Somebody died. Ah, good, I'll get to see—I will see." It was only the quick grasp of Karen that turned him around and sent him scurrying back to me.

"No, son, you really don't want to see. It's only books that make you want to see. It's only TV that makes you want to play this part. This is no book, no TV; this is no movie. This, John Jackson, is my yard in Jamaica, and this is real. This is life. You have not had your tonsils out—you have not jumped out of an airplane in a parachute—you've not fought the Vietnam War—you've not survived the destruction of the Challenger. You are alive. You are visiting your grandparents in Jamaica. That haunting scream of death is real. This is your grandmother, June. Your grandfather is still in the house. Your mother, Carlene, is still sitting there on the golf cart. You are looking at me. I am the one who is white with fear and has trembling legs. I am the one that is alive. The black man lying just off the yard by the green is the dead one, the one with his head cut off,

3

and his arm almost cut off. John Jackson, you and I are the two sitting on the green overlooking the Cinnamon Hill Great House framed by that beautiful Caribbean Sea—watching the white owls swirl and the johncrow land only too near—vomiting our guts out."

I am American by birth, but part Jamaican by the grace of God. Though I live in Tennessee, for the last twelve years, a love stronger than I makes me cling to an island rich in akai-bread, fruit, flowers, and the love of God. A people who love to serve have chosen to let me in some way be one of them and their lives. If facing death on the North Shore is part of this, so be it.

I remember jasmine—that's how Jamaica smells to me—jasmine—and I think of all kinds of fruits and vegetables that just hang on the mountains, and the jams that feed you. God has blessed these people with needing fire only to cook, for it stays warm there most of the time. These are the good things. Then I remember the machete, the one near the head—near the body—and the arm.

They also clear the jungle with the machete.

And that particular machete cleared my head a little.

P.S.: A man up on top of Mount Zion had many mahogany trees. The story goes that three men poached the trees and were reported by the owner and were to be jailed. Thinking that the farmer had reported them, they hunted him down. He is the unlucky man that we found lying near our yard as we were leaving for the airport to return home from a trip to Jamaica.

A CUTTING EDGE

I have performer friends who won't ever give a picture of their children to anyone. *You're too uptight, I used to think. My goodness, people want to see you, to know you. You can't lead your life thinking there's a poor crazy waiting at every corner. There isn't a poor crazy waiting at every corner, not* every *corner . . .*

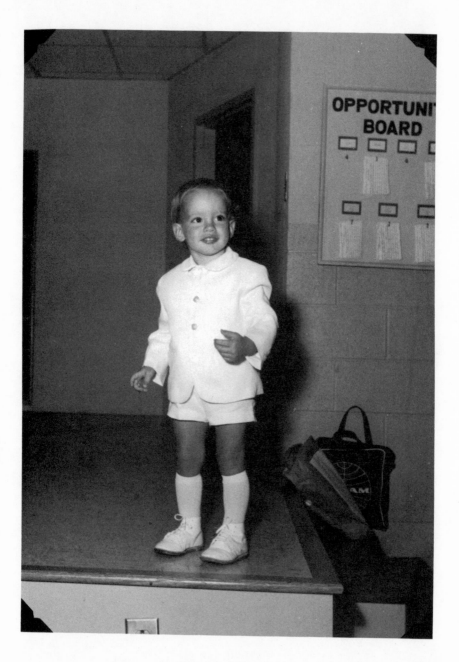

John Carter Cash.

My husband's name is John R. John for first. R for Rah (Hurrah), R—Rajah (King of country); R—Ramrod (of his family), R—Rasputin (sometimes a holy term), and R for really Cash; R for Rich—a little rich; R for ready—for that he always is, ready. John Ready Cash—ready—first in faith, and ready to love and defend his family, of which there is a pretty good group. My two girls, Carlene and Rosey; his four girls, Rosanne, Kathy, Cindy, and Tara; and our own John Carter Cash. I find myself wife and mother to this bunch.

"John, I think I need a gun."

"Are you afraid?" he asked.

"Yes, I am afraid. But not of this bunch."

It was a simple envelope—the words printed—but straight to the point: *Put $250,000 in a plain brown paper bag, and drop it at the exit of I-25 [and some street I don't remember], if you value the lives of your kids. Do it today.*

I get a call from Carlene at school.

"Momma, Rosey called me to ask how you were. Only, Mother, I know my own sister. It wasn't Rosey, Mom, and, by the way, there was a long black limo following me and my date last night. Thought I'd better tell you that, too."

Later that day, the FBI pick up some guy exiting I-25 and jail him, finding he'd written another extortion note to a banker in town. No danger now. John Carter's too little to notice. Carlene and Rosey arrive home, sure some movie scout is after them in his long black limo.

Shades of the Tennessee Highway Patrol, the FBI, and John R.—Bibles and family and friends, Kris Kristofferson and Shel Silverstein, make their way to New York City to perform at Madison Square Garden. The plane stops on the runway—door opens. The captain: "You'll have to take your family out of here, Mr. Cash." Seems someone wants to kill us all again. There's no place like New York City to hide, especially if it's Madison Square Garden and you've only about one hundred police, along with your own jim-dandy spotlight, singing your best in the front of nineteen to twenty thousand fans in the great big superstar days of ole J.R. and J.C.C. and J.C.C.

They didn't kill us. They only said they might, just a voice somewhere from the night.

I started carrying my Swiss army knife. Yanked out the longest blade, threw it like "Tonto"—bull's-eye. Took seven stitches in the palm of my hand.

It made a nice impression on me.

IT'S ALL IN YOUR MIND

People who are basically healthy think a toothache or tight shoes are painful. You can be kind to them, be forgiving, but you don't ever have to listen to them complain.

Steve Goodman.

They were all lying. There was no such thing as pain. It was only a word from the dictionary that you used for an excuse to take dope. All the world operated this way except me. I never hurt. I never had pain. They were all lying. I never took dope—until I was forty-five years old.

I now find myself better qualified to talk about this subject. I took the highest top of the point out of Lake Tahoe and skied all the way down: to the right, to the left, around that tree, around that log—jumped that little hill—bend, bow, and burn that hill, I did. I skied all over that snow like a pro. I was wonderful. I was past moving. I had done all of this, but always on flat water—in a lake—never on snow.

I am now in a position to talk of pain. I had to have a pill for pain every night—one for my back, one for my legs, and one for my head—all aspirin. Becoming an expert on pain, I came to grips with life. Years go by, but the good ole pain stays with me. All muscle joints and bones are in sympathy with my aching back. Now the front hurts. Operation is the only way—doctors—Mayo Clinic—hysterectomy—complications—operation again—intensive care—no female parts left—depression—ninety-four pounds. Two hospitals later: staph infection and a hole in my stomach.

I got out my Bible. I prayed to die. I would have felt better. I went to our home in Florida. I had a hole that wouldn't heal in my stomach. My friend, Steve Goodman, had a hole in his head and his chest (where he applied medicines daily). He had leukemia.

We sat on the dock and soaked up the sun. I read my Bible. We walked. I prayed.

We waited for the holes in our bodies to heal.

I lived.

Stevie died.

I am ashamed to speak of pain.

Rosey.

MOTHER/ DAUGHTER

Sometimes it seems that the road to any kind of knowing is too rocky and hard to be worth the knowledge. I walked a road like that with John, and we made it to the top, bruised. I walked another hard road with my daughter. I'm ready for an Interstate.

Hello, June. It's Elias."

"How's Vegas?" I asked. "John and I miss you, Elias."

"Me, too. It's Rosey."

He didn't have to say it's Rosey. I knew it was Rosey. "Is she alive?" I asked.

"Yes, but I've got her here in Vegas. She arrived yesterday, carrying her guitar, a bottle of Jack Daniels, and heaven only knows what was in her purse."

This was my Rosey. "My precious Rose," I always called her. My youngest daughter—the biggest heart of all with a problem to match. This time it's cocaine—the nose just can't take any more.

John got me a Lear jet, and Peggy Knight and I flew all night to Vegas. She didn't want to see me. She should have been in Pepperdine University. She should have been in Strasberg Acting Class. She should have been studying in Los Angeles. But she was here in Vegas out of her head on cocaine. My precious Rose was "zonked."

Mothers sometimes push too hard. Rose took a while to collapse. We left for London. She drank—she married—got beat up a lot—drank some more—went to jail (not for long)—wrecked one car, then wrecked and burned her next car, and went to jail again for three days where she punched out a dyke.

"Hello, June, it's Anita."

"Omaha, you say."

"Yes."

I didn't have to ask.

"It's Rosey," she said. "Please pray. She just stopped breathing," and she hung up.

Another hospital—another drying-out period. But somehow the I.V. got pulled out and the blood backed up—blood all over her— she's in shock—she just died—the blood is everywhere. Jesus, Anita where are you?

The phone went dead. Fifteen minutes later Anita's voice came through over the howling of several tornados, "She's all right now. Rosey is alive now."

Came home a little sadder—a little bluer—a little older—a little truer. If I had a dollar, I'd give it a go—and I'd lay it all on the Wildwood Rose.

Rosey said to me, "Momma, God gave me an ulcer so that I couldn't drink, He sent me Tiffany [her niece] so that I wouldn't drink, gave me asthma so that I couldn't smoke, then gave me ulcers in my mouth so that I wouldn't eat. I will soon be perfect." Today she's back in college.

Oh, for the courage of the Wildwood Rose.

First Battalion Staff. Sponsor, John Marshall High School.

CHILD STAR

Now I know that every teenager dreads being different. I know that. And I know that being different isn't really a bad thing. But, oh, Lord, I wish I'd known that when I was a teenager.

We were both fifteen. I was Valerie June Carter and she was Joyce Blair Dobbins. We were seniors in high school at John Marshall in Richmond, Virginia. I just wanted to be like all the other girls in that school. I wanted to go to dances, have dates, see the ball games, go to pep rallies, hang out after church with the crowd, meet at Hotchkiss Field to watch football practice, have an ice cream soda at the drugstore, and ride home on the streetcar with my best friend. I wanted to do all those things Joyce did and all the other lucky girls. I wanted to be a sponsor—there were only ten—for our Cadet Corps. Joyce was going to be a company sponsor; she was the girlfriend of that good-looking captain, Joe Purcell.

My life was a little different. Oh, I got to dance a lot—but not with boys very much. My dancing was done on some high school stages at night, where I hoofed away—one of the silliest-looking vaudevillian jigs that a girl could ever do. I wore pantaloons out of necessity—because my feet were flying in all directions—mostly up over my head—and I was a part of our variety show, "Mother Maybelle and the Carter Sisters." Between singing Carter Family songs we sang pop tunes. I played the Autoharp, Mother Maybelle played the "Wildwood Flower," Helen played the accordion, and Anita stood on her head and played the bass fiddle. We did old vaudeville skits and we sold pictures for twenty-five cents apiece.

While everyone was dating, I was busy riding everywhere in our old Cadillac, setting up the P.A. system, and taking up money at the door.

While everyone was having a soda, we were singing away on the radio and planning another show for the next A.M.

I could sometimes see the football field as we went by—and get a glimpse of the cadets as they strutted their stuff—thinking in shades of West Point. My life was a failure at fifteen. Joyce was a sponsor for that good-looking Captain Joe Purcell, and I didn't even know a good-looking captain anybody.

Joyce and I had one thing in common. We were both Christians—and we prayed a lot. I prayed not to die, night or day, on the highway, since we drove so much. I prayed to be happy with my family and I prayed for our health. God had seen to it that I had all of my needs, so we decided to pray that God would hear a prayer from a little fifteen-year-old. Just to know that if two were gathered together in the name of Jesus, and asked for anything, He would see that we got it. It was so simple. We prayed. We believed. We prevailed. And the only good-looking, unattached captain in that Cadet Corps walked up to me and, without knowing why, Captain Bobby Spires asked me to be his sponsor.

The miracle of prayer; that good God heard such a silly little girl and her insignificant prayer. I never forgot it.

The House of Cash.

SIGN IN, PLEASE

John Denver's fans thought he was too stand-offish when he put up a sign on his Rocky Mountain High's: Private. Please Go Away *or whatever it was he said. I wonder what his day was like before he put up the sign.*

Her name was Violet Topian. She was a friend of mine.

Armando Bisceglia is our chief security guard in Tennessee, where we live. It sounds so harsh and cold to talk of guards and dogs and someone between you and your front door—always someone with you—someone who says, Sorry Mr. and Mrs. Cash aren't in town today, or they're asleep now, or they can't see you today, they can't see you or the hundreds of people who are there, or could be there, trying to get over the fence, past the guards, through the front door, just to say hello to your face. They say they know you well; you are their friend.

Lots of people are in Nashville, taking a bus tour, driving their cars out to see where Johnny Cash lives on the lake. They come by the road. They come by boats, and some fly over in small airplanes or sometimes balloons. It's a wonderful thing that they have somewhere in their lives heard of you, or seen you on TV enough to feel as if they could come in and sit down—and I'd fry the "taters" and cook them cornbread for the beans, and we'd just visit the whole afternoon.

Armando, please don't forget to put the book out for the tourists to sign. Please call on the terryphone if I'm home, and you think they are family or friends. Please put their names down; give it to me. Don't miss a one—it could be someone special. I have heard of fans and friends turned away time after time from other stars' homes, and I remember once thinking, I wouldn't mind seeing Elvis again. We used to be friends. We worked together—but something made me stay away from that gate in Graceland. I think I was afraid that he wouldn't remember me at all or I'd be turned away. So I never stopped at that gate. I simply remembered the times he just drove to my door and we were friends years ago. I mashed his bananas and peanut butter—fried his eggs well done.

Every time I've gone to Richmond, Virginia, since I was a child, I've looked in the telephone book for the Violet Topian name. I asked my friends if they remembered her. No one did. She was the first Armenian that I ever knew. She was a friend of mine. We ate my first Chinese food together on Wednesday afternoon after school. I remembered learning that my Lord Jesus probably spoke

Armenian. I expected her to spout the New Testament at any minute in Armenian. She never did. I looked for her every year. She did not make the ten most important girls in high school. She was not the prettiest, she was not the most talented. She had very curly hair. She spoke with a slight accent. She was a friend of mine. I haven't seen her for forty years.

Armando, please don't forget to get the people to sign the book, if I'm away, and put an address down please.

By the way, have any of you seen Violet Topian? She is a friend of mine.

John with his parents, Mr. and Mrs. Ray Cash.

JACK AND JOHN

It's funny how a sound or a smell can flash a whole memory into your mind. A Christmas tree or the ocean or chili on the stove, and you're right back to that rainy day or good party. It's a nice bonus—most of the time.

He was a child of God. A man child. Wisdom beyond his years. He did not know hate—it passed him by—and you wonder how I know him when I never met him. It took fourteen years for him to die.

You see I know his brother well. I lie with him at night. He shivers in his dreams and sometimes calls for Jack, but the angels sung a louder song and Jack ain't coming back.

I know Jack was good, kind, and pure. He left ahead of time John tells me as he weeps. There's no way for him to know how I know Jack so well. John tells me when he sleeps.

Jack fell into a saw in a workshop at school and died within a week. He was fourteen—two years older than John.

I smell napalm when I hear a helicopter blade. I smell the burned flesh and the powder from mortar shells. It's a long way from me and Saigon in January of 1969. I'm flat on my back in my bed in New York City. Now I am chilling, and the TV is flashing the news. It's now March 25, 1986. It's the Gulf of Sidra, and they are sending the S.A.M. missiles. The carriers are all in the Mediterranean Sea. I don't really care whose Gulf it is. I don't want to smell the burning flesh again. I wonder where the *El Paso* is.

The escort tender ship for the carrier, Coral Sea. I wonder where Captain Roy Cash, Jr. is. Somewhere on the *El Paso*, next to the carrier, near the firing S.A.M. missiles and the dead. Some are dead, I know.

A doctor once screamed at me in Long Bend Air Base in Vietnam. "Help me, Help me!"

"I'm no nurse," I said.

"I don't give a damn who you are. Help me with this boy."

I took a young man in my arms and tried to soothe him.

"You'll be all right. God is with us."

But his flesh was burned with the napalm and it stuck to me like glue. It hung to my arms—my army fatigues that read CASH on the left breast. I took part of that boy home with me.

I'm afraid again. The name CASH does not read JUNE this time. Oh, God, deliver our nephew, Captain Roy Cash, and all the boys from the awful smell of burning flesh—napalm—and war!!

LESSON IN A CAR

*There's always something or someone to re-
mind you of how far you ought to go, even
when you're just passing time on the long ride
in from an airport.*

John Carter Cash.

He was asleep on his pillow in his room. His feet stuck out from the foot of his covers and hung three inches over the foot of the bed. His thick red hair tassled down over his eyes, but it did not touch his collar. (Good old Good Pasture School, I thought. Thank God for the dress code.) He wore a silly, contented smile on his lips and he was dreaming, I'm sure.

I'll just stand here and maybe I'll understand him a little better. He looked like most young men his age. For fifteen, a lot taller, and bigger, I guess, and I suppose the rest of them sleep in a different fashion. His hands clutched the neck of his dream guitar that still hung around his neck—and his fingers flew over the strings. He picked hard and fast with the right hand, as it fought to obey the challenge of the left hand, playing some imaginary tune with no sound. Isn't that sweet, I thought. He's probably playing the "Wildwood Flower" like his grandmother Maybelle Carter. But come alive now. That is my dream, not his. The only reason we aren't hearing the ringing of the strings and all the heavy metal in concert in the country is that he's still asleep. His biology book is on the floor, covered up with guitar strings. His geometry book is still in the car.

Come on, John Carter, I prayed. You can do better in biology. You can do that geometry. I know you can. You're hanging on by a hair.

But then I stop and think, and, if they gave a grade in guitar, that would be an A; and the thing that blows my mind is that there's always an A in Bible.

Teachers, it'll come together, maybe, anyhow, biology, economics, and then the "Wildwood Flower."

"Do Ernest Angsley, John Carter. You sound just like him. You're so clever and funny."

It was a great way to entertain ourselves riding to New York City from the airport. John Carter was about twelve, and his voice squeaked and called out the sounds of a TV minister, Ernest Angsley, slaying imaginary people in the spirit, and it was wonderful fun. We all laughed.

It was like an explosion. I thought I was shot. We three had been seated in the back seat of our rented limo. I was flanked by John and John Carter. I was happy and safe in the middle. There was lots of glass—there seemed to be millions of tiny slivers of very sharp glass covering me. My arms, my face, my body—my lap was full. I was literally covered in shattered glass. There was none on John or John Carter, just me. We couldn't understand it. Then John reached down, grabbed a big round rock from the floor of the car, and started running fast with that rock in his hand, scurrying after some tragic-looking, tall, hungry figure. They both ran. The police ran. I sat in shock, afraid to move for fear I would be cut to pieces with the glass. John caught his man and rammed that rock in his face, yelling, "Is this your rock?"

He could speak no English. He was French and hungry. I don't think he knew who we were. He may have thought we were the full-bellied capitalists, and, in all his frustration, threw the rock through that symbol of wealth and power—in his protest. I was the object covered in glass—and then I remembered that John Carter was doing Ernest Angsley. Only in fun, we said, but beware. When someone speaks the words of God, do not jest. Even a hungry Frenchman could be Jesus—with a rock in his hand.

GANGRENE

There are poisons that contaminate the body, and we know there are poisons—good and bad—we've used on our soil. I've seen and heard minds poisoned by fear and hate, but I'd never really been on the receiving end of mind poison until that night in an Atlanta parking lot.

Carlene Carter and June—Glad you're back in Tennessee.

It's so green—not a healthy growing new green of spring but a sick gray milky green, dripping into the bottle that hung suspended from somewhere under the covers. The mucky green clung to the sides of the bottle that imprisoned it forever. Oh God, help us forever, please. To be able to funnel it into the bottle was a miracle, because all this poison was hidden waiting to devour the small egg of life—and the poison had chosen to secret itself inside the fallopian tubes of my daughter, Carlene. She lay lifeless— barely breathing. She was not white or red—she was the color of death and dark gray. The pretty, bouncy blond hair clung to her head, oiled from the roots to the ends as if something inside was putting forth all its efforts to keep anything, even a hair, alive.

The fifty-year-old woman in the next bed called loud for a bedpan. "I'll be having the bedpan please—now!"

A small nurse appeared slowly carrying an ancient tray of some sort that did not appear as if it would ever in this world become a bedpan. Her nurse's hat was strange—tall it was—like none ever seen before. She did not give the lady the bedpan but moved on to a young girl down the ward who was vomiting at the time.

"Nurse, shouldn't you check my daughter, please?"

"No, she's unconscious, Ma'am."

"I can see that!" I screamed. "What's wrong with you all here? Can't you see how sick she is? Doesn't anyone care?"

"You shouldn't be here, Ma'am."

"Oh, but I am in here, and I will be in here. Can't you see this is my little girl?" Only she wasn't little anymore. Small, yes—lying against the pillows—sick and small. "And I will not leave here. I will stay," I ranted at her. "How long has she been out?"

"Seventeen hours, Ma'am."

Oh my God, I prayed. The ward held twelve beds and sick ladies, but none so sick that they couldn't even ask for life, save my daughter, Carlene.

I remember thinking I'm going to wake up—I know I am—and she will be all right.

The green was growing in the bottle. "Is that what peritonitis looks like," I asked.

"Better out than in," the nurse said.

"Where's Nick?" I screamed.

"We ran him off. You can't stay in here, either."

"I didn't fly all night from San Francisco, around the pole to London for you to get rid of me that easily. You will have to remove me bodily," as I wrapped my leg around the table end, prepared for a fight.

She gave up on me and moved nearer to the bedpan lady.

"I want my daughter moved to a private room."

"There are none, Ma'am. This is England. Socialized medicine and all, you know."

"Did the operation go well?"

"I think so," said the nurse.

"Doesn't anybody know anything? Is she going to live?"

"We think so," she said.

I wanted to scream. I wanted to cry. I wanted to ask Nick what had happened. I wanted to pray. What had happened to the little child that Carlene and Nick thought they might be having? I think somebody should answer these questions. "I want the best specialist we can find in London. I don't want my daughter to die."

I sat by the bed for another hour—just looking at her, praying and hoping—and slowly the long double eyelashes fluttered, and the eyes opened a little. She could not seem to focus her eyes. She looked all around me—said "Nickie, Nickie," then "Oh, Mama, mama. I've been dead," she said.

We were to play the Circle Star Theatre out of San Francisco when Nick's call came. "It's Carlene. She's terribly sick, June. The doctors kept giving her the wrong medicine, and she was pregnant in the tubes. England is slow—they sent her home, but by the time we got her to the hospital, the tubes had burst and she had gone into peritonitis. We may lose her."

I ran for an airplane and started the long journey toward London. It was the longest flight I could remember.

"I'm here, Carlene. Don't worry. You're going to be all right."

"Oh, mama, mama. I'm so sick. My tubes burst, and the last thing I remember was the doctor rolling me down the hall screaming, 'Get me some help. Those idiots have let this girl die.' "

Then she went out again. She said, "It was like a long tunnel."

Carlene had married Nick Lowe and moved away from Nashville

34

to London. That's sad for a daughter to be so far away. She and her daughter, Tiffany, had left us crying in Tennessee, and her son, John Jackson, had stayed with her ex-husband, Jack Routh. My John says a boy needs his daddy—but then a girl needs her mom. Here I was a mom—and couldn't do much of anything.

Carlene opened her eyes and said, "My house is a mess."

"I'll fix it," I said. I'm sure my son-in-law, Nick, was as afraid of me as I was him. He was a rock-and-roll producer, as well as a singer—and to him I was a die-hard puritan from Tennessee. We would have to adjust to each other. He came in with friends, and we breathed a sigh of relief that Carlene was awake and the terrible infection could be put into a bottle and thrown away.

Nick and I went home to Shepherd's Bush. They lived in a four-level house with a brightly colored door. The first floor was a recording studio where the likes of Dave Edmunds and Elvis Costello moved about, bouncing the boards off the floor and walls.

Secure that Carlene was going to recover, the nosey mother-in-law sets out to clean and spit polish the neat little house in Shepherd's Bush. I cleaned with Tiffany's help and polished all. Got a maid, Pervis, to come over to nurse Carlene when she could come home from the hospital—ran my "Hoover" as Nick called it. You might just hear me on some big hit record that Nick was producing at the time, hissing away, spraying polish on the furniture or sucking up dirt with my Hoover. I liked this world of rock-and-roll pretty good. We got to be good friends.

"Hey, Nick, the truck's here."

"Here?" over the bass and drums. "Here?"

"Yeah, here now. Bring Martin Belmont with you. He's tall (6 feet, 4 inches) and strong. We'll need him to help."

"Help? Help what? I need him to overdub his guitar on this record."

"It's only an armoire."

"Armoire? I don't need an armoire on this record."

"It's to hang clothes in. I need it out of the truck, up three flights of stairs to the empty bedroom."

"You want me to take these hands that finger the electric bass for solid beat and sound to pick up that great big piece of furniture on that truck and carry it up those stairwells?"

35

"That's the idea—I can't lift it. I hurt my back years ago. Lifting this same sort of thing."

"Oh come on, Martin. She's not going to stop chattering until we move this huge monstrosity."

"Don't worry, son. I'll just throw this dude in the oven. Then I'll be back to boss."

Nick, "What's a 'dude'?"

"Don't you know anything, Nick Lowe. A dude is a chicken with all the condiments (here being onions, potatoes, and carrots). You'll learn."

"I don't want to learn," with the "she'll go home to Tennessee look" glazed in his eyes.

"I'm stuck, Martin. You'll just have to carry more," rounding the turn on the second stairwell.

"I'm stuck as well, 'Mate.' " "This is not a 'stuck as well mate' move. You'll have to get it out, otherwise you won't be able to get the other one by this one."

"The other one? There's another one? (Defiler of guitar- and bass-picking fingers.) I could really get around to knowing what a 'dude' is, slaving away in the old MacDonald—you know—mother-in-law dear. What's that hissing? You aren't cleaning the furniture again, are you?"

"Yeah, Nick. Just a little squirt here on the second level."

"Martin, this woman is cooking 'dude', and we are in peril here. This thing (armoire) could fall on us—squash us into pulp. Who wants a pulp producer with no fingers to turn the knobs on the dials in the studio?"

"Maybe she'll be gone tomorrow," Martin squeaked out after the second armoire cleared the last flight of stairs.

"Now the bed," I said.

"These things have a bed?"

"Yeah, Nick. A smaller bed. Carlene cannot come out of the hospital and dive into that king-sized bed on the top floor, recessed way down below the flashing Kleig lights. She's sewed up. That is definitely not going to work. She has to have a bed she can sit down on and gently crawl into."

"There, mother-in-law dear (on my heels). By the way, is the dude done?"

When Carlene came home—almost well—I'd become a pretty good rock-and-roller. I love Nick Lowe. We were buddies. "I'll have to learn more about what these children do and how they live," I said. I cried, leaving Carlene, Nick, and Tiffany in London.

"We're going to see Carlene in New York. You'll come with me. She's well and she's playing there somewhere."

"It's the Ritz, a rock club."

"That's easy," I said. "Carlene, Helen, Anita, and I will come to the club—get a table down front and watch the show."

"No mother, you'll do like everyone else. You'll stand down front and scream and yell. Please don't wear a big fur coat."

"Oh," I said. "No fur coat. All right, no fur coat."

We cut Carlene's picture out of the *Daily News*. Saw Carlene's lay-out by Helmut Newton in *Harpers Bazaar* from Paris. I was a proud mother of my rock-and-roll daughter.

"I'm going into Atlanta (working on the CBS movie "The Baron") to see Nick." Bob Wootton, Fluke Holland, and Roger Morton (our bus driver) made the trip with me to a nice little club outside of Atlanta. We were prepared to scream and stand up. Nick provided us with a table. This is great, I thought. I'm going to get to sit down. We tried that a little while. It didn't work. You had to get back into the stand-up-on-the-table routine in our world of rock-and-roll. I was getting good at screaming and rocking and rolling. The kids all looked young and like nice kids. Bye, Nick.

In the parking lot on the way out—I'm sipping at my Coke in a paper cup—a policeman grabbed me by the arm and took away my Coke. "Give it back," I said.

"What have you got in it?" he barked at me.

"What do you think I've got in it, sir?"

He took the cup, drank from it.

"That's Coke," I said, "Or can't you tell?"

He proceeded to taste Bob's, Fluke's, and Roger's drinks, one by one.

The irony of the situation is that I don't drink at all. Neither does W. S. Holland. He's never even tasted alcohol. Bob Wootton does not drink, and Roger Morton never drinks on the job. So this was what prejudice was. We were feeling the brunt of just liking rock-

and-roll music. We had done nothing, yet we stood accused of something, I guess.

"What are you doing here?" the officer said.

"I've come to see my son-in-law. Now, if you don't mind, sir, move your car so I can get my bus out of here."

Peritonitis is a poison that sets up out of infection. It seals itself off and becomes gangrene.

Gangrene sometimes takes on other forms. The poison is not in the stomach, but in someone's mind—other than mine—for those who don't understand rock-and-roll. There are no little green bottles catching the refuse. Some of us are just mothers that love their children and love to tap their feet to the music. We've entertained Tom Petty, Elvis Costello, Paul McCartney, Bob Dylan, and James Taylor in our home. They are nice people.

Carlene has moved back to Tennessee. She now sings with my sisters, Helen and Anita, and myself. This is the brand new Carter Family. We've made a new album, are working on a new radio show, and are part of the Johnny Cash Show. We plan lots of things. There is no joy like the joy of singing with your family. Come see us, Nick Lowe. We love you. No gangrene here. I'll cook you a "dude."

SUPPORTING PLAYER

Why can't I be Moses—and he hold up my arms? Why do I always have to be like Aaron? Why is it always me? John always wins the battles—just like the children of God. He's always Moses. The minute he lets down his arms—we all go down in defeat. But that is what God said. I guess as long as Aaron holds up Moses' arms—we will win the war. The minute they let go of his arms, the Israelites are defeated again.

God give me the strength to lift his arms and be satisfied with that. It's just that some of us aren't good for anything except holding up an arm.

Two "Carters" and a Cash.

HIS NAME WAS
DR. TURPIN

You shouldn't blame the people of a whole country because of a "diplomatic incident." There are a lot of things you shouldn't do.

Well, my TV set is sharp in color and having itself another war—Nicaragua, the Falklands, Grenada. We watched them all with glee. It's easy when you're in comfort. They kill and maim, then win the war. It's free for me to see. The Gulf of Sidra is on today. Twenty-seven went down on a boat—twenty-seven more. Gosh, they do it all by rate.

How awful, June, don't you recall? Don't you go back about two-and-a-half years ago when the Russians shot down that Korean plane? Three hundred plus died. It wasn't some other place. If it had been on TV, it could have blown up in your face.

His name was Dr. Turpin. He was a friend of mine. Actually, he knew me well—better than most that I had ever known. He took care of me, and most of the time he had a better view than other men, except John, because he was my gynecologist. He checked me over inside and out. He took good care of me—for John and I had planned a trip to Russia. We were to perform for two cities, Leningrad and Moscow. Only for very special Russians who were great Johnny Cash fans. It was a trip we had longed to make.

We were sure that somewhere we could find people in Russia who did not want a fight and who we might sing our songs to and in some way mend our diverging paths of understanding. Surely, we could help.

"Hello, Dr. Turpin. Please. It's me, June Carter Cash. Gotta run in fast for my checkup. We're away on our trip to Russia. Will he see me, please?"

I hung up the phone and fell down on my knees. I couldn't talk. I couldn't speak.

John said, "What's wrong with you?"

My Dr. Turpin won't ever see me again. Not in this world—maybe in another life.

He and his pretty wife were near Japan on some Korean plane. Oh God, John. The Russians shot them down.

John cancelled our Russian dates in September 1984.

THE SECOND TIME

When Jesus fell that first time, He found the strength to get up. I think we all have the strength to get up that first time. It's the next time that's bad; when it's all happening again and there's no top to the hill and no strength left—you've used it all up. You haven't, but, please Jesus, no third time for me.

Tired and busted down.

et Go and Let God" sounds pretty. Sounds easy.

You can do it. Let her go . . .

"Let Go and Let God." Those are the words they give you to hold on to in the Betty Ford Center, if you're one of the many who have a family member with the disease of chemical dependency.

It's not news to tell you that my husband, John, has a chemical dependency problem. They know it in the good ole U.S.A. They know it in England, Ireland, and Scandinavia. They write books on it in Germany—and all the unknown languages seem to get it said without my help. Oh, well, here I go again. Let's not talk about him—let's talk about me. A man who drinks, or takes drugs, is having a wonderful time. He is out of his head—his gourd is full—he is flying—his star is in the heavens—for a time. It is the codependent that is the sickest. We are the worst of all. We have sunk below the sinkhole—we are in the mire. We are down somewhere in the crevice and the crack. We are in the Ring of Fire and the flames are going higher.

We are also very angry. We let go—so that we can live. It is very dangerous to let go. I know.

BETTY FORD COUNSELOR: Let go.

JUNE: Sure, I let go. It's gone. There is nothing to hold on to. Now what do I do? I did it before I got here. I am now somewhere in my forty years in the wilderness. I am hanging on a cross.

BETTY FORD TALKER: Jesus beat you to it, June.

JUNE: I know how He felt. There is no place that I don't have pain. It used to be in my heart. Now it's everywhere. Come on, God. I'm letting you—I let go. Where are you?

BETTY FORD PERSON: Let go.

JUNE: Go where? This pain is worse than death. There's no road back. You see. I'm even arguing with God. I'm not having a good time.

BETTY FORD LITERATURE: Let . . .

JUNE: Shut up. I don't want to hear you. You see, it is so dangerous to use—for us all. It took me a long time, and John as well, to crawl back up a cliff with no rope—a path with no stepping stones—a way with no will.

Yet somewhere—from out of the goodness of God, we made it. I hope you never feel the pain. I would not wish it on anyone.

NATIVE BORN

I think I'll be part Indian. I'd like to have the power to be in the decathlon, be Jim Thorpe, and throw the shot put by the hour, or I'd soon be Oliver LaFarge and win the Pulitzer Prize. I'd put on my Olympic medal and try it on for size. I'd take my prize money and I'd put it in the bank; then I'd write myself a check and I'd buy myself a tank.

I'd be Ira Hayes, driving with my bulldozer blade. I'd run one hundred miles an hour and I'd show you how we're made. I'd push you like a boulder and let you watch me carry my load, 'cause I'll be the rich Indian on the nickel and not the fat one by the road.

I've seldom met an American that doesn't claim to be part Indian—on his mother's side—or father's side. They all will claim that honor. I've also noticed they sure like to pick their Indian.

ON LOCATION

We were making a movie in the Holy Land. We were really there. We even had time to sightsee, and naturally, as many family members as could, came with us. I wasn't sure any of us would live to tell about it.

John on location in Israel.

Come on down," John called from the valley; it was winding its way amid tall cliffs of fifty feet in the air, pure chalk tops, bottoms, and lots of caves—holes and nowhere in between. We were near Sodom and Gomorrah, not far from the Dead Sea, and, standing from my vantage point of fifty feet in the air, the top of my cliff looked secure for me. I didn't dream it would crumble.

"How'd you get down there?" He seemed to have been born there. Since morning, searching for just the right shot of our Mary Magdalene (me, in *Gospel Road*—movie of Christ—my brainchild and my dream). We had crew, friends, family, and enough faith to take on Cecil B. DeMille. I wonder how old Cecil B. would have gotten down that cliff.

The top of the cliff was level. A few bushes and me, daughter Rosey, Reba, and Mariel Curtis all waited patiently for God to part the Chalk Mountain—crack out the steps for me to make my grand way downstairs through the likes of an ancient Sodom and Gomorrah.

"Over here," Shaygrah Ben Josef called. This head just seemed to stick up out of the Chalk Mountain. He looked as if he had been buried neck deep—no descending, no ascending.

"How'd you do that?" I asked.

"It's easy. The chalk is very dusty; it crumbles inside this mountain. There's lots of passages."

Oh, great. Rosey and I ran with the elasticity of a worm. We'll just cut down through that little hole.

Where did Shaygrah's head go? It popped up another fifteen feet away, like a little prairie dog. We all wormed our way into the chalk and were popping up now and then as a jack-in-the-box, high on that Chalk Mountain near Sodom and Gomorrah.

The crews set up here in the valley. They had come another way, starting at daybreak.

I know why Shaygrah Ben Josef is called Major Shaygrah Ben Josef. He probably won the Six-Day War all on his own. We were more into "Ole Chalk Mountain," making our way through what I consider to be the results of the last of Sodom and Gomorrah. There must have been fifty feet straight down, and a few stalagmites pushing up with three or four stalagmites protruding here and there. We followed—mole fashion—on our way down.

Shaygrah, balancing on one toe, lifting an arm over his head called up, "Sit here on my hand."

"Who me? Me on your hand?" It's only a ten-foot jump to that hand. Good old agile me will give a little pounce, and I'm sure to set my bottom flat on that hand that is reaching to heaven.

"Rosey!" I shouted, "go first." She's agile. The bones won't break so easily. She is the strongest. Straight down—there was no way to go, but straight down.

The upper chalk crumbled away, and I prayed for shades of some combat training from some other life to bounce out of my subconscious. I would give a little leap—land on Shaygrah's hand on my rear—crawl down his body over Rosey. That's where she was also crawling at the time. All this with him balancing on one foot—and the chalk melting and falling away.

"Hold on to both my feet, Rosey. Don't let go, Ben Josef."

"Why'd I want to let go? You'll fall," he said. "Don't look down."

We now had two bodies, Shaygrah's, Rosey's, and mine crawling down to make a third. I grabbed everything that was sticking out and looked up and descended the human mountain.

Mariel and Reba also crawled down that human chain.

The Israelites won the war. Shaygrah never let his arm down. He just kept calling. "Here, jump on my hand. I'll hold you."

"What do you suggest I jump there with?"

"Your posterior." Some more Hebrew words that no one could understand. Then, "Oh, well, jump on your *ass.*" That's the same in any language.

So jump on our asses we did, on Shaygrah's hand, crawled down his arm, his body, his hulk of a frame into the second chain, which was Rosey, then me, then Reba, and a screaming Mariel—one by one.

We literally walked on air down that hole in a fifty-foot chalk hole—clinging now and then to somebody's belt—then nose, their hair—both arms around a waist. We grabbed anything that wasn't falling at the time.

We lay prostrate—all five of us—on the floor of that chalk cave looking fifty feet high to a round hole of light and wondering what in the world we were walking on coming down.

A Shaygrah, a prayer, but we were there.

SMILING IRISH EYES

Printer's Alley in Nashville was a rough place on Saturday nights. Boys with too much beer in them looking for trouble and finding it right away. Shoot, how bad can a pub in Belfast be, John? Let's go meet the Irish. Only keep them out of Printer's Alley; they'd wreck it.

Ireland.

It's one of the finest old pubs in Belfast. All along the front there is beautiful tile and scenes of a time past for the Belfast of today—this was the pretty one, the Crown, the lottery, where you lose your money. Then the number 40, then the number 38. All lined up in a row on the corner. Just across the street from my safe and secure fortress of the Intercontinental Hotel. My vantage point was made even more secure being perched on the ninth floor from my living room. I wanted to visit a pub. I'd never been in an Irish pub; and anyone who has a husband who has written the Irish ballad "Forty Shades of Green" should just get her foot inside to somehow feel the homing device that pulls all the young and old Irish toward the pub for a pint—a brotherhood that you were born into and no one could tell you about. If it ever hooked you, you were drawn there just as sure as if you were a young salmon fighting the mighty rivers, rocks, falls, etc. that take you back for your death to your spawning grounds. The pub was a part of your life classes— your mother, brother, sister, daughter, and wife. I pulled up my chair and sat about seeing what the great and wonderful calling card of the three pubs had to offer. I noticed the young at first—about twenty-five of them. Maybe six or eight motorcycles pulled up in front. Most wore jeans and leather jackets, with boots for kicking. Let me tell you. Make a young Irishman mad, and he will knock down the po-lice, the owners, the bartenders, and the one with the aprons and sticks. There is blood streaming from his long hair—and he can kick the closed door with the velocity of a Gatling gun. Then, even higher, above the transom, that boot will fly, and he'll be pulled away by a fullback. Then there'll be something said that wasn't just right and off he goes again toward them, kicking, punching his way through friends and foe alike. We now have fifty to seventy-five who sympa-thize, but there seems to be an army from within, thirty-eight or forty, punching out any long head of hair that comes through. There's only two ambulances there now. I wonder just how bad the one on his knees is—and the one lying down. Worse still—I can't make out if that's glass and beer—or glass, blood, and beer. The streets are lined with young, yelling, screaming girls, crying and pulling, telling their side of the story. It's time to leave for our con-cert now. Here I go. John and I are singing "Forty Shades of Green" at the top of our voices. They all seem to know that song. Both sides.

I sing it through the bikers—they join in. The ones with the clubs keep time with the clubs—a short reprieve now, as we all hear the words. Sing—sing—you hear the words.

I close my eyes to picture the Emerald of the Sea from the fishing boats at Dingle to the shore of Donagha Dee. I miss the River Shannon and the folks at Skibbereen. The moorlands and the meadows with their "Forty Shades of Green."

THE TALENT
SCOUT

On stage, you often will pick out one face to play to. It's a subconscious thing; you pick out the one you sense really likes what you're doing, and it gives you a boost to that next energy level. Any time I look at my nice capped front teeth, I think of one face in a Nashville audience.

June as "Aunt Polly Carter."

That poor little man has a hole in his shoe. I could see that from my vantage point out on the Grand Ole Opry stage. He was seated in the wings on my left side, leaning back in an old chair.

Gosh, I hope that chair lasts through the night. He tips it back, riding it, as the spindly legs strained to hold the burden of him. Not that he is heavy—it is a bad chair. His feet cross and the half-soles on his shoes still sport the worn places all the way through. He holds a camera in his hand.

Wonder where he got that good camera that goes *click, click, click* all night for the Grand Ole Opry. Not so much for the Grand Ole Opry itself, the lenses seemed to always be pointing at me.

He's squatting down by the back curtain now, still aiming that camera in my direction.

I catch that as I kick and twirl my way through a fast flatfoot with a little of Nina Farnoff thrown in. There's nothing like the freedom of a hard-driving mountain dance, with a little ballet step now and then to give it some "couth." Mercy, I wish he had snapped that shot with me on my toes, instead of my foot bent like a double-edged jack handle.

I'll try a smile. Why am I smiling at that little man that I don't even know? The one who looks as if his hair is bent and curled like a corkscrew. He looks as if he has just pulled off the head part (the one that looks like a big brass bulb with a glass in the front) of a diver's suit. He looks as if he has just ascended the depths of the Gulf of Mexico—somewhere near Tarpon Springs, Florida. The only thing that's missing is the sponges in his hand. Yeah, that's it. He's removed his diver's suit and he still has on his clothes that he wore under them. His good suit that needs pressing. I really think they don't pay those sponge divers enough. He's bound to be Greek.

I'm playing my Autoharp now, and peeping around to see if he's still there. Yeah, he's still watching. The microphone is sending out the sounds of my mother, Maybelle Carter, and sisters, Helen and Anita. It's a good sound tonight—Chester Atkins is weaving his magic on the guitar, and I'm singing to the top of my voice. There's five thousand people out front of the stage, yelling and having a wonderful time. Looks as if I could have picked one face out of that

57

crowd. Why do I have to keep watching that little man over there with the camera? It's a good camera. I hope he didn't steal it.

I've swung on the curtain, told my funny stories for network radio. We've all taken our turn singing. I wish sometime Anita would give me the high part. Why does she always float around up there on those notes like a balloon in the air? Maybe it's because I can't reach it. Yeah, that's a good reason enough I guess. Chester keeps telling me to "move back, you're too close to the microphone, June." That don't even make sense, does it? Helen, Anita, Mother, and I all sing a song. Why does he make me stand two feet behind them? It's hard enough to be part of four Carters with eight healthy mammary glands fighting for space in front of the mike.

That little man knows exactly what I'm thinking! That's scary. He's even putting it inside that little camera—*click, click, click.* I'll dog it right on past him as I leave the stage. What if he speaks to me? I don't have time to talk to him. I'm expecting someone. My New York agent, Harry Kalchiem (also my godfather), sent me a telegram. Someone would be there to see me. I can't remember his name. It's on the telegram in my purse, in the ladies toilet, past that strange little man.

I'll hold onto Chester's guitar cord and follow him—that's what I'll do. And as I pass that little "dude," if I don't have guts enough to keep walking on, Chester will yank me free of this strange force that makes me watch and wonder about this man.

Here we go. What's happened to Chester Atkins? I'm standing here in the wings talking to a wiry-haired little man with holes in his shoes, who has taken at least fifteen rolls of film, when he could have used that money to buy himself a new suit and shoes. I've also got Chet's guitar cord still in my hand. Oh well, I'm stuck. If necessary, I'll use this cord to wrap it around this dude's neck. He's got a nice smile. I don't think I'll have to use it.

"You want to get something to eat? I'd like to take some pictures of you."

"I might have a little time." Just like that—the words popped out of my mouth into the atmosphere—right into that dude's ears. I had no control over what I said—and here we go. I stopped at the toilet to get my purse on the way, and we went to a little restaurant around the corner from the Ryman Auditorium on Broad Street.

"You're taking a lot of pictures," I said.

"I like that," he said.

We'd both had a sandwich, and I reached for my purse. I'll probably have to pay, I thought. I opened it, casually took out my telegram to see who I had an appointment with. Mustn't do that. Can't let Harry Kalchiem down, I thought.

"By the way, what's your name, sir?"

"Kazan," he said. "Glad to know you."

I opened the telegram. The bottom line read, *His name is Elia Kazan. Love, Uncle Harry.*

We spent about a week talking of a project that he wanted to do. A movie of some kind. We visited. I introduced him to people in country music, and we were friends.

He said, "Have your two front teeth capped. Study dramatics— not here—in New York City. Get the best drama coach. Get out of here for a while. Go to school. Study speech. Study dance. Improve yourself. Do whatever you want to do. You can do it. I'll introduce you to Sandy Meisner."

I did it.

His best friends call him "Gadge."

I remember him with pride as I think of *East of Eden, On the Water-front, Cat on a Hot Tin Roof, The Arrangement*—the great Broadway shows, the books, the movies. I never had the nerve to call him "Gadge," but he was a friend of mine, and I still watch and look to see what has happened to him. This little man with holes in his shoes never knew; I never got a chance to tell him in the last few years. He changed my life, and I wonder if he even remembers my name.

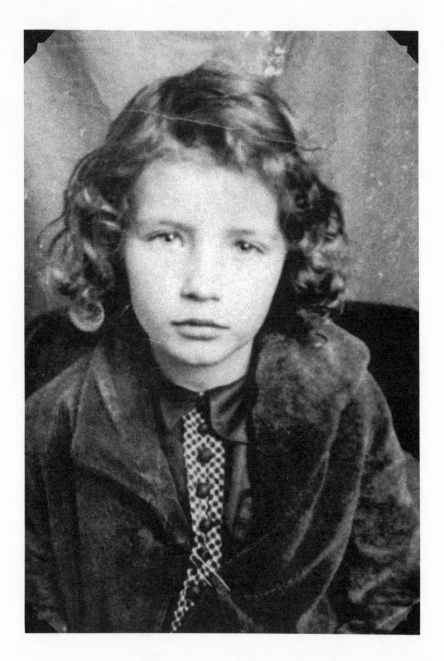

June Carter, five years old, Maces Spring School.

VALERIE JUNE, MACES SPRINGS SCHOOL

My mother warned me about so many things. She was right most of the time, but, of course, that had nothing to do with paying her too much mind.

Don't you know you can't just play with anybody? These mountains are full of all kinds of people—clean people mostly, but don't you know that there's a few that have never seen a wash rag? Watch to see if they're scratching their heads. That's a good sign.

Now that seemed like a bad sign to me. Anyone that just kept scratching their head in the Maces Springs School just might have a big family of varmints living in the wonder world of hair on the head. I really liked that little Vermillion girl. She had wonderful black eyes and eyelashes that seemed to grow in rows on top of rows. That was wonderful.

"I'll swap you a light bread and sandwich spread with 'mater sandwich for that biscuit with ham," I said. She was ashamed of her brown sack worn thin by the daily trip to-and-fro to the top of the mountain. The same lunch sack, but a different biscuit in it. That biscuit always had meat in it. I guess sometimes it was possum, squirrel, ham, or groundhog. But it sure was a big hunk of meat, and that biscuit was a real big wad of a biscuit. I liked biscuit.

The light bread truck came once a week to Neal's Store. Mommie would send me with a dime for the bread and another dime for the salad dressing. Sometimes we would pull off five bananas from the big stalk that hung in the front window. The stalk would be hung green, and I'd wait daily until that good Virginia mountain sun would stream through that wide window with the thin outside bars to get the bananas just the golden color that would give us a treat; or better still, if we had vanilla wafers, we'd pool our bananas and make that mouth-watering three-inch-high meringue with custard filling banana pudding. My lunch box was tin with a thermos for milk in it. There was always a napkin just over my two peanut butter crackers. They were all on top of the Spam sandwich at the middle. I used to think Mommie put the 'mater sandwich on the bottom just to squash it.

Don't touch anybody that's got a sore on them. Look between their fingers, that's a good sign. There's germs everywhere.

Get in the cement tub. Take a bath again. Wash. Wash. Wash your hair, put on clean clothes. Brush your hair, shine your shoes. Get ready for school. Brush your teeth, use mouthwash. Be sure to pour Lysol on the toilet seat. Put a big scoop of lye down in the toilet.

Hold your breath when you go in the toilet. Don't play with the dog. He's got fleas. Be careful in the barn—there's chicken lice in the hens' nests.

It was a rough day on me that Monday, I guess, but I was sure Mommie had her own list of things for little girls to do to protect them from the dangers that come with our valley in the days of depression.

Hi—
Say the prayer
Get the bucket
Go to the well
Draw the water
Read, write, study
Drink out of the dipper
Play basketball on the dirt court
Run to ask Daddy if he'll buy us a net for our hoop
Put your head on your desk
Eat lunch
Get your Bible out
Ask Mommie if the teacher, Miss Hilton, can ride in her car to
  Bristol Saturday
Name the presidents of America
Be tired
Walk a mile home

I feel a lot better now. I've got a big biscuit with some meat on it—groundhog, I think. I like groundhog. Be sure to bring back paper sack. I hope the black walnuts don't punch a hole in the sack.

I can see that little Vermillion girl. She must be halfway up the mountain. I can see the little tin lunch box in the setting sun. She's sitting under a tree. She's eating the peanut butter crackers, the Spam, the mashed 'mater sandwich. There she goes, still carrying my tin box.

Here I come, Mommie. I'm the one with the biscuit and groundhog in her stomach, the black walnuts in the brown paper sack. Oh, by the way, Mommie, you'd better borrow some kerosene and sulfur from Mrs. Vermillion in the mountain. I'm also the one with the itch and the lice in her head.

June and Chet Atkins.

ME AND CHESTER

Chet Atkins is one of the all-time greats. There is nothing that man can't do with a guitar. I am still lost in wonder when I think about his giving the little Carter girl lessons. I wonder if he'd ever take his kindness back. He wouldn't.

You put on a thumb pick first [on your right thumb]. The rest is easy."

"Oh, really?"

"You hold your guitar like an ordinary person. Your thumb hits the first string, near the hole in the guitar. Remember to hit the string with enough force for one to hear it loud and clear."

"This is easy."

"Oh, I forgot to tell you. If you want to hear some kind of a melody, you must also involve your left arm, hand, and fingers."

"Oh."

"The good ole left hand will now hang your thumb over the top neck of the guitar. Your remaining fingers will grasp the guitar neck somewhere near the screws and pegs that the guitar strings are attached to."

"I can do this."

"You must cut your long fingernails."

"What?"

"Yes. Now that your left hand is holding the guitar neck near the screws and pegs, with your freckled fingers sporting your nubby-looking fingernails, you feel a little more secure."

"I feel just like a guitar player. My hand has a grip like a vise on this dude now. I'm on to it. I think I'll stand up with my guitar."

"Put the strap around your neck."

"I don't have a strap yet."

"Sit back down. Don't move, just hold the guitar in your lap."

"This is easier anyway. I'm better coordinated this way. My right thumb is rarin' to go."

"You won't be going anywhere."

"Oh."

"Hang that left thumb over the neck of that guitar. Way down. You've got to grip that first string hard."

"I got it."

"Hit your down stroke with your right thumb."

"Ouch."

"Put your pick back on."

"My pick?"

"Your thumb pick."

"There." *Splock!!!*

"The sound is not supposed to be *splock*. It's supposed to ring like a bell. Be sure your left thumb is hooking over on the string on the first fret. Hit all your strings on a downward stroke with the pick on the right thumb. The first five of them, that is."

"What happens to this last puny little string, the one that really sounds bad—like it's out of tune?"

"Oh, you must take your left hand. The index finger must grip the neck, then hook down under the neck and grab that little string on the fret."

Splock!

"No, no. I think you're out of tune. Tune it."

"Tune it?"

"Yeah, get all your strings tightened and screwed until they sound right."

"Tighten and screw?"

"Pick with your right thumb, hook with left thumb."

"Tighten and screw." *Splock. Double splock.*

"I'll tune it."

"I could have done that. I just need a little time to hear it properly. My ears have been stopped up. I've got it. Here I go."

Loud roaring *Splock.*

"You're doing something wrong. That's supposed to be a G chord. That isn't a G chord. I know one when I hear it. That is definitely not one."

"Oh—my left thumb slipped off. It was somewhere near the left index finger for moral support. I'll hook her around again. I know now why the left thumb darted off."

"Hooked left thumb. Big string on top of guitar—clutch left index finger on smallest puny string, also left hand. Fret. Don't forget it's the first fret."

"I got it—I got it."

"If you've got it, why can't we hear it? We don't got it out here outside your brain. Our ears must hear what you're doing. You're muffling your strings."

"O.K. Brain. Hands and fingers. Message coming. Hook, grab, clutch, unmuffle, pick—there—ring.

"A chord, that's a chord. I've made a chord, Chester Atkins."

"You've made a G chord."

"I knew I could play this guitar, Chester. I'd like to play 'Walking the Strings' tonight in Sevierville, Tennessee, on the show."

"On the stage tonight at our concert—in two hours from now?"

"Yeah, this is easy, Chester. What do I do now? Where do I put these other fingers—the ones on my left hand? And I want to use all the fingers on my right hand, too. How do you get your right thumb to pick the strings going and coming in the same lick. You all won't have to back me up. I'd like to do it by myself. I don't need you out there confusing me or Anita drowning me out with her big bass fiddle. Helen's accordion is too loud for my solo. Mother Maybelle would flash me a tragic look if I accidentally *splocked* one string. Just because she plays everything in a case, she thinks all the notes should ring clear. I guess we've shown 'em, Chester. Chester—hey Chester. My left hand's in a cramp. I can't seem to get it unclutched off the neck of the guitar."

"I think I feel an asthma attack coming on."

"You don't have time for an asthma attack."

"Maybe Mother Maybelle will teach you 'The Wildwood Flower,' or the 'Carter scratch.' Anyone just learning to play the guitar should begin with the Carter scratch, June. She's your mother. She loves you. You're a Carter. You should start pickin' a Carter family song. I think I'm beginning to wheeze."

"I'm on to it, Chester. You just announce me on the show. After your asthma attack. You saw—you know I can do it. I am playing this guitar. You haven't heard one *Splock* out of me in the last three minutes."

INGRAFTED

Rosemary Edelman was my first friend in New York. How she put up with this green girl who knew it all is past wondering. We've stayed friends, but I still don't like hot water with meal balls, and she still doesn't like gravy.

Little Junie Carter.

You look pitiful, Rosemary—standing there alone on that corner. I saw you in class."

"I'm lonely. It's New York City."

"You have wonderful clothes. I like your big white hat. You have beautiful eyes and milky-white skin."

"I want to be an actress."

"Me, too. I thought you already were one. Are you having a hard time, honey?"

"Yes."

"Come home with me."

Jesus, I thank you for all the blessings. I thank you for life, I thank you for helping me find a good apartment in a good section of New York, so I won't get mugged and raped. These were the main concerns of my gentle little blue-eyed mother named Maybelle, as she waved good-bye to me, getting on an airplane with all my suitcases. It was still like a dream, but here I am in New York City, living, studying, dancing, taking speech, cooking, making interviews, and also taking care of my daughter, Carlene. I was so busy that the pain of a broken marriage hardly had time to creep into my life again.

And Jesus, I thank you for all the good vegetables I've been able to find here in the city. I thank you for all this good. In Jesus' name—Amen.

"Why do you have to pray as if the world was in its last twirl, and you and I were getting thrown off, June?"

"I'm trying to avoid hell, purgatory, the lake of fire, home of eternal damnation—Rosemary. It's way down below heaven."

"Heaven?"

"Yeah, the home of God and Jesus, Rosemary. Don't you know anything?"

"I know about God and I've heard of Jesus."

"Heard of Him? Is that all? How can you hear about God and not know Jesus, and the Holy Ghost? They're all the same person."

"Same person? I understand, I really do. I know why you give thanks for the food. What's this we're eating now? It's pretty good."

"That's country ham."

"Country ham?"

"Yeah, I brought it from home. You can't get it in New York City. My daddy killed these hogs."

"Hogs?"

"Yeah, pigs. You *know* with the cloven hoof? Don't worry about it, it's clean now. God fixed all that in the vision of the sheets."

"What's sheets got to do with me eating pig?"

"St. Peter fixed it, you know. St. Peter—Cephas built the church on a rock. He fixed it with God. He cleaned up the pig."

"Oh, maybe I'll just have a biscuit."

"No, have some gravy and grits. These eggs aren't any good. New York City doesn't have any gravel and dirt for the chickens to peck in."

"June, do I have to get up at six o'clock every morning and eat gravy and hear about God?"

"Sure, we'll do a lot better in school. We'll think better, work better. Always eat a good breakfast. It's the only way. You're too skinny. Put a little weight on, girl. What's the matter with you? You'll probably have a sinking spell before noon."

"It's noon, and I'm having the sinking spell. I'm the one that feels awful. I need chicken soup. I called the store and look at this stuff, Rosemary. It's hot water with meal balls in it. I don't need meal balls."

"June, this is chicken soup."

"Where's the chicken? Why have they put a hole in my biscuit?"

"It's not a biscuit. It's a bagel. Hey, Ga-Ga's coming by."

"Who's Ga-Ga?"

"She's my grandmother."

"Hey, that's wonderful. I'm going to get to meet your little ole grandmother."

And in walked Ga-Ga. The first thing she said was "I don't like this damn wallpaper."

Ga-Ga wore diamonds and furs. She also looked a lot like Elizabeth Taylor. Ga-Ga was not like any other grandmother I had ever seen.

Rosemary was my very first friend in New York City. How Rosemary put up with this green girl who knew it all is past wondering.

Her father, Lou Edelman, gave me my first network television lead as an actress in the Jim Bowie series for two shows. Her mother, Rita, gave me an added desire to be a gracious lady. Her sister, Kate, helped me get this book published. Rosemary sometimes got up with me and had coffee while I had my monstrous breakfast. She listened to me pray and talk about God. I learned a lot about how life was for a young girl raised in Beverly Hills, California—a young Jewish girl. We were from two different worlds and they went on spinning. Our two worlds have dove-tailed now, and we both get up at six o'clock in the morning to pray to God. We've stayed friends, but I still don't like hot water with meal balls in it and she still doesn't like gravy.

Cast of Stage Coach. *Left to right:* **Kris Kristofferson, Tony Franciosa, Willie Nelson, Elizabeth Ashley, John Schneider, Mary Crosby, Johnny Cash, Waylon Jennings.** *Kneeling:* **Anthony Newley, June Carter Cash.**

THE BABIES

They aren't really babies, you know. They're grown men—Waylon Jennings, Kris Kristofferson, Larry Gatlin, Joe South. I didn't give birth to them, but they're mine, whether they like it or not. I've claimed them a long time. I never stopped until now to wonder what they think of me. It really doesn't matter. I'm gonna keep on caring for them. I've worried about them, prayed for them, sometimes in the night without knowing why. My good husband would wake from a sound sleep to ask me, "Who is it now?"

It could have been any one of the four—Waylon, Kris, Larry, or Joe, but this time it was Waylon. "John, it's Waylon and Jessi. I don't know what's the matter. I only know that they're in trouble, and I can't get off my knees." Sometimes that would last all night long. How come I chose to pick Waylon Jennings from the time we first met in 1956 as my charge for life? I would worry, wonder, cry, be pleased, be sad over his life, until today. I took him through all his marriages, his kids, his first record contract, his highs, his lows, and now to his precious "Shooter," and Jessi.

Waylon, you are a friend of mine. You've been a friend of mine for a long, long time. Waylon, I think you were seventeen. You were young and mean, but you could sing. You always treated me fine. And Waylon, you are a friend of mine.

And Kris, your jeans sure were ragged. I know I could see his knee sticking through his jeans really good. The spotlight would sometimes pick up his knee. Sometimes it flashed on Shel Silverstein's head. The spotlight #1 held Johnny Cash in the light circle of center stage at Madison Square Garden with me to his right. About twenty thousand people, and the thing I remember most was Kris's knee and Shel's head—applause. A baby boy, fame, a good friend who hitchhiked from Nashville with his knee shining through his lucky blue jeans.

He is really a poet, you know. Our very best country songs of the day have come out of that head with the mind of a genius. No one knows it yet, but my husband would fix that. John loved Kris, too.

Thirty-five thousand people were in the crowd at the Newport Folk Festival. It took a healthy push to get the lucky blue jeans out on that stage with Kris inside shaking. "I can't play the guitar. I can hardly carry a tune." Who cares! We had the sounds of "Me and Bobbie McGee," "Sunday Morning Coming Down," "The Good Times." We heard the melodies through the night and the sound of that gravelly voice. His picture was on the front page of the *New York Times* the next morning.

Once, when John Carter was five, a jeep turned over. The doctor said "He has a fifty-fifty chance to live." I was on my knees in front of the intensive care unit. I could not get up. I opened my eyes to see the ragged old lucky blue jeans that hugged the floor beside me. We beseeched God to listen. He did. I can rememer Larry's knees beside me on the other side. John was trying to gather some strength from his good friend, Roy Orbison. There was a man who had suffered the death of his wife on a motorcycle, the death of two children in a fire next door—home, wife, and children—and he had the strength to hold his friend, Johnny Cash, in his arms to tell him that it will be all right. That John Carter will live, and live he did. He is now pushing six feet three inches with a size thirteen shoe.

Kris was up—he was down—the women ran through his life, and he lived a life apart from us. I did not forget him. We could see him once a year, and it was as if we had said good-bye the day before.

"What are you going to do now, June, that Kris and I have straightened up? Who are you going to pray for now?"

"I'll just give thanks that you've had a good day."

He sat on a stool at church. A small church. His face beamed; he sang with a love of God that I understood. We were soul mates.

"You've got to hear this boy sing, John."

"I don't have time. Get Larry Butler to listen, too. You've told me Kris could sing. I hope he sounds better than Kris does."

"Take the time."

"There is no time."

"Who's that playing guitar on my session?"

"That's Larry Gatlin."

"Larry who?"

"From the stool at church. He had to make a car payment. He can sing parts."

"I don't need anyone to sing parts."

"He can write."

"I don't need anyone to write."

"You need someone to write another song for the *Gospel Road* movie. His voice is the voice of an angel, if the angel happens to be a man. He has a gift of throwing his voice just anywhere he wants it to go." Larry, you can be one of my babies.

He did *Gospel Road*, "Help Me"—Las Vegas—John called him The Pilgrim. We ran in.

"It's on the radio," someone said. "You and John are getting a divorce."

"That's terrible. Did they say who was getting custody of John Carter?"

"John Carter, my foot. I've come all the way from Los Angeles. I haven't slept a wink. Who's gonna get custody of The Pilgrim?"

We both claim custody of The Pilgrim, as he counts "All the Gold in California."

"Mercy, John, it's Joe South. He's dying. I know he is."

"How do you know? You don't even know him that well."

"Yes, I do. I know 'Walk a Mile in My Shoes,' 'Rose Garden,' and 'Games People Play.' I can't help it if God wants me to pray for Joe. I'd rather not. I don't even know him that well."

"It's Joe's time now. It's 5:00 A.M., and you're down on your knees again. How do you know it's Joe South?"

"I'm choking to death. He is, too. I know it."

When I awoke, I felt as if I'd come back to life again. Not a wonderful life, one with a hurt head, a difficult time for breath. I was barely hanging on.

Did Joe make it?

The paper read: *Joe South picked up on Malibu Beach, nearly drowned.* He is lucky to be alive.

I still worry about him. I worry about them all—these babies who did not ask me to care. They may not have even wanted me to care. They have done everything I thought they could. They have survived the pull of this world. They have wives and their beautiful children. They have achieved fame in a world that does not give it away.

Through their glory—their trials—I have cared about my babies. I wonder if they know. I haven't had the right opportunity to tell them I am proud of them. Even if they wanted me to go away—even if they chose never to see me again—they are still my babies.

It's a lot easier to have four full-grown new babies—if your husband considers that they are his also.

John does.

THEY CALLED
HER A COMMIE

I've heard all the arguments about nuclear power; how it's past discussing, it's here; how it benefits an economy; how it's so good for us, and we're just too dumb to be grateful. Well, I don't think it's past discussing. The folks in Chernobyl didn't discuss it either; they didn't have a chance to.

John and June in cotton fields in Dyess, Arkansas.

I t's a fail-safe program. There is no way we can accidentally start a nuclear war. There are many things to protect us. We have missiles that will shoot down missiles before they ever land on us and kill us all.

Is that so?

Why worry about the danger of or seriously take to heart the power of nuclear energy? We need the power for peaceful purposes—for energy to run our big cities, our factories, and our extravagant way of life. We cannot maintain our present standard of living without these nuclear plants.

Is that so?

I watched in horror as I saw the plans in some newspaper for the nuclear power plant to begin in Hartsville, Tennessee.

Maybe they won't start it. It'll take millions to build it.

They are building it, you know. It's only about twenty-five miles from home. My good friend, Dolores Seigenthaler, rebuked them and told them to go away. They did not. They called her a Commie.

What does it look like? It's provided many jobs for the area. Lots of people need work. Don't say anything, don't do anything.

I won't. I didn't. Dolores stood alone, she got 'em. It'll take a long time to build it.

I don't understand about nuclear waste. I don't know where it comes from. I see it go by in unmarked trucks. They're taking it out of state and burying it in Alabama. Thank God. They'll take it somewhere else.

There are three big tall stacks in Washington State. Tall stacks on Three Mile Island, too—Red Wing. There goes another truck. They're burying it deep.

Are they?

There's no danger.

That's good.

There was an accident on the highway. A lot of men sealed off the roads. They carried Geiger counters. It's all cleaned up now. It's all right now.

Is it?

They said it won't be long before Hartsville goes on the line.

I don't want it to go on the line. What's on line? It becomes a working plant. Uranium core, all that stuff. No one really knows.

Don't they?

There goes another one of those trucks. They all have tarpaulins on them.

Why?

I don't know. Do you?

What's meltdown?

I think you get a fire from the nuclear core that won't go out.

No one can get hurt. They use robot arms to pick that stuff up. The Geiger counter goes off, if you get any of it on you.

Does it?

Hartsville still isn't on line. Thank God. These nuclear plants dot the United States and Russia. They're very secret.

Why?

They harness uranium, and it becomes a power, as a cloud. Almost as the power of God. The nuclear bomb with Russia and her big red button—us and our big red button.

We won't push it.

Good.

Do you think they will?

I don't know.

Carl Sagan talks about the fires and the dangers of a nuclear war. A nuclear winter—the end of life as we know it on this planet.

Lord, have mercy on us all.

They may not know just how much damage is done from the accident at Three Mile Island for twenty or thirty years. We'll wait and see if the children's hair falls out. If the young women abort. If the weak die sooner than soon. If the old do not see their last days.

It wasn't too bad.

Wasn't it?

There's a dark cloud again. It hangs over Kiev—the farms and the Russian people. They have blood in their veins just like we do. They bleed, they get sores on their bodies—inside and out. The cloud moves—over the Balkans, over Scandinavia, over Europe.

They showed them planting seeds twenty miles from Straunika. Everything's all right. I saw it on our spy satellite.

Good for us. It's just a little fire in the core. Just a little meltdown.

Is it? What have we done? What are we doing? No one pushed the big red button, and the horrors of the fallout drift across the ocean. From one to another we spread the poison.

Do we?

What ever happened to the front porch swing, the rocking chair, the homemade ice cream, the giving it to God? I don't know. I can't see it for the nuclear winter—the cloud that we're spreading without ever pushing a red button. I can barely see the Hartsville plant.

They stopped working there
I heard someone say
But they could start working
Most any day
So Dolores I'm ready to stand
We'll scream for them to stop
We'll jump up and down
And do a rabbit hop
Your John can put it in the paper
My John can sing of the energy faker
Because fake it is and good it is not
It's a deep gut feeling that I've got
So my John sings of the water isn't water any more
Your John's editorial still reads of civil rights and nuclear waste
While banging on the president's door.

The early days of radio. *Left to right:* **The Carter Sisters, Cousin Joe, Uncle A. P. Carter, Mother Maybelle, Aunt Sylvia Carter.**

THE DEPRESSION

Tuberculosis was an uncontrolled killer when I was growing up. None of us knew what it was except that it showed no quarter. It was one of the things Mother Maybelle warned us of. My cousins on the hill were warned about it too, but it took one of my young cousins, and escaping it took two more.

Don't go in that room. Charmie is in there."

"Why can't I see Charmie? She's beautiful. She's sixteen, and everything I want to be. Her eyes have three or four rows of wonderful eyelashes—raven hair. Why is she so pale?"

"Don't ask questions."

"I didn't like that funeral. The one where they buried her brother, Dewey. Why did my heart hurt so? Why did Aunt Mary and Uncle Charlie, Coy, Stella, Elna look so sad? Why was Stanley sitting in the chair all the time? Why couldn't Charmie come?"

"Be quiet. You're too young to understand. Don't drink out of that glass. Help me boil these dishes."

"Why are they all so pale and worried?"

If I could live on the mountain when Daddy built the wonderful house they're living in now. I love the sun porch down one side and the front porch. A house with wire on the side porch to keep out the flies. It was like a mountain retreat where you could sit in the rocking chair and drink lemonade.

"Why did they move off the island? They had good jobs—all of them. I like Stanley's new Cadillac, Coy's Hupmobile, their roadsters. I like the way Charmie, Stella, and Elna look in their tall boots and jodhpurs. I like the goggles that Coy wears on his head. Why did they leave Kingsport and just quit to sit here, grieve, be silent, and worry, Mommie?"

"You're too little to understand."

Charmie is dying.

She's too young to die. She's never even been married or had kids or lived her life. She is the prettiest of all of us.

She'll be pretty in her coffin. I don't want her in the coffin. My heart hurts.

They're leaving. They're all going. Maybe Arizona. The air is good in Arizona. It's fresh there. There's work in New Mexico and California. They can get a job in Kingsport.

They should burn their house on the island. The walls are infested. First Dewey, now Charmie, and Stanley looks real bad.

Uncle Charlie's hair has turned white, and Mary still works like a bantie rooster.

"Why aren't Coy, Stella, and Elna sick, or Uncle Charlie and Aunt Mary?"

"I don't know."

"Mommie, what's the matter?"

"It's T.B., June. Tuberculosis."

"That's bad, right?"

"That's bad. That's death."

"Oh."

I stood by the tobacco barn and watched those cars pulling out. They had Coy and Stanley driving. They looked great. The girls wore their riding boots and jodhpurs. Stanley coughed. Daddy tied the last crate of chickens on the rear bumper of the Cadillac, just before the trailer that hauled the tent, the pots and pans, pillows and blankets. They tied everything in and on those two moving cars that made up the convoy of Uncle Charlie Bays and Aunt Mary, on their way to fresh air—new jobs—and California. How beautiful they looked. We watched from the tobacco barn, halfway up Clinch Mountain. We could see the empty house with the sun porches to the right and the convoy moving slowly down the hill to the county road. Mommie and Aunt Sylvia cried. I worried. My heart hurt.

"It's a letter from Uncle Charlie."

"Where are they?"

"In New Mexico. . . . Get the Lysol. We'll try to clean the house on the mountain."

"Can anyone ever live there?"

"I don't know."

"Why didn't someone get the doctor?"

"They did."

"Why didn't they live?"

"I don't know."

Another letter.

"Charmie's dead."

"Out there in New Mexico?"

"No, California."

"They're not old enough to go back to dust. They're all under twenty. How can they bury her out there away from Stanley and Dewey?"

"They have to."

"I don't like it."

"I don't either."

I dreamed the chickens flew out of their coop.

They're really gone. They ate them all—and peaches. They're eating peaches. They're also picking peaches.

I wished I had some peaches.

I missed the Uncle Charlie that had that wonderful, handsome face with the white hair. I cried for the eighty-seven-pound Aunt Mary who had the strength and stamina of a giant. I missed Coy holding me on his lap and bouncing me on his knees. I missed Cousins Stella and Elva. They were pretty.

The cars are gone.

Where'd they go?

They had to sell them.

Are they all dead now?

No. Some survived. Uncle Charlie died at eighty-five, Aunt Mary died last year. She was 105 years old.

LEAVING THAT LONESOME VALLEY

There was never any talk about whether or not I'd be part of the Carter Family. I was part of the Carter Family, but to join the singing and strumming Carters I had to learn to do something people thought was worth coming to town for. It was a good thing the rest of the family knew what they were doing.

On the Barn Dance, WRVA, Richmond, Virginia, 1946. *Standing:* Anita. *Sitting, left to right:* June, Mother Maybelle, Helen.

I don't even think she can sing."
"How do you know?"
"I've never heard her."
She's always in the barn with the chickens, milking the cows, hoeing the corn, that's her. Stuck like a June bug behind her daddy on his new Harley-Davidson. That's her upside down in that biplane flying with her little goggles on beside her Daddy in the open cockpit. That's her gigging the frogs in that flat-bottom boat in the Holsten River with her daddy. That's her rear end sticking up off the bank of the pond there by the jar of tadpoles.

That's June.

Yeah, Valerie June. The middle one. Helen is the one playing guitar and singing harmony. That's Anita with the Shirley Temple curls singing like a Swiss Bell and yodeling above us all.

"Maybe June could learn one song."
"Yeah."

"Sit still. You're gonna have long curls."
"Me?"
"Yes, you. You're gonna play this Autoharp."
"Me?"
"Yes, you. You're gonna sing 'Engine 143'."

Along came the FFV
The swiftest on the line
Running on the C & O
Just twenty minutes behind
Running into Sewell Headquarters on the line
Receiving their strict orders from station just behind.

"Good. That's good, June. Sing the rest of it."
"There's more?"
"Well, I know they had a really bad wreck—and there was a fire—and somebody named Georgie said your life may yet be saved.
"Something about a railroad track and laid in a lonesome grave."
"I'll just tell it. I don't know it all. I'll just pause now and then. The people will know I'm swollering and they won't dream I don't know the song."

"June, I can't take you back to Texas with me to sing on the radio with you pausing and telling half the song. Helen can play. Helen can sing. Anita can sing. Open your mouth. Think Aunt Sara and Mommie. Think Uncle A.P. and sing."

"Sing?"

"Yeah, sing right. Don't sing wrong. Play the Autoharp at the same time. If you're gonna be on the world's largest radio station with us—we'll need some kind of a miracle."

"You can play the "Wildwood Flower," Mommie. Why don't you play your guitar for me while I sing and talk."

"You can't just know one verse of a song and expect to get paid."

"Get paid? They pay you for singing and playing?"

"Yes."

"Well, I'll certainly change my life here. Give me that blamed Autoharp. Give me that wraparound pick. Give me my microphone. Give me my check. I can't believe it. Helen, you just wait until I start. Anita, you wait, too. I want my part first.

"And you can have what's left."

GOOD OLE GIRL

That's little Junie Carter on the radio. The one that talks too much; the one with her family, Mother Maybelle, Helen, and Anita. That dignified group. Where'd she come from? She's the same one that swings on the curtain, that works the lever for Chet Atkins's vibrato on his D'Angelico guitar. Why does she say "Martha White Fleur?" Why can't she say "flour" like the rest of her family?

Do you know she can put her stomach anywhere she wants to put it? She can swing out over the audience on the curtain from the stage. She can kick the ceiling and throw her ballet shoe to hit anyone she chooses in the audience—right between the eyes?

She's the same little June Carter (on the radio) they mention in *Tattoo* and the *Garden of Sand*. Why did they do that in them nasty books? She sure ain't nasty. She's a good ole girl. I think I'll go to Nashville this Saturday night and see if I can see her.

"You gonna talk to her?"

"No. I'd like to pinch her."

"You a dirty little ole man?"

"No. I'm a little ole lady."

John, June, and the Carter family with Larry Gatlin and the Gatlin Brothers.

MAKING AN
APPROACH

We'd caught a plane, all of us. The "Johnny Cash Show" had to be in Erie, Pennsylvania. We'd had breakdowns, car failures, late trains, but we'd never bounced off the ground before while still in an airplane. Do you know, we've actually gone back to Erie, Pennsylvania?

My nose stuck to the window of the glass. It mashed there, stopped by some invisible thing that pushed it flat like a button between my two blue eyes. God, can you see me now? This is me, Valerie June again. I'm the one with the button nose against this glass straining to see you there. Where are you? I know you're there in the fog somewhere. The fog is thick, and it's good you can't see the fright in my eyes or ole button nose in my desperate effort to get you to manifest yourself in some angel form through these white-gray swirling layers of black fog that have engulfed us all. I need you, God. If God could have seen any better than I that morning over Lake Erie, He would have seen a DC9 in desperate trouble trying to find the airport in Erie, Pennsylvania. God could have seen many faces glued against the windows as that airliner tried desperately again to find the airfield.

My eyes picked out all kinds of faint images in the fog. All kinds of things that did not resemble one airport light—no runway—no trees—nothing—just moving, waving, elusive dreams of fog. Nothing tangible was there. I knew we were near the ground. The nun sitting near the Gatlins—Larry, Steve, Rudy, and LaDonna, was saying the Lord's Prayer out loud. I removed my nose from the window, glanced at Reba (John's sister). She was smoking hard, and her hair was wet from sweat. I held John's hand, said a prayer, and thanked God that I had, for the first time in his precious life, left our son John Carter home. I glanced at my mother and sisters, Helen and Anita, Marshall, Carl Perkins, Fluke Holland, Robbie Hardin, brother, Tommy Cash—all in a fleeting moment. I said good-bye to them all, silently—and began to say quietly.

"Yea, though I walk through the valley and the
shadow of death, I will fear no evil . . ."

We seemed to be sideways and still moving—more down toward the ground. The plane balked, reared, tried to right itself, and I felt the left wing hit the ground. The front end shot up as the pilot fought to control all that power—and I could see the runway. It was coming fast from the right window about one hundred feet to the right of us. We were approaching it right side first and about two hundred miles an hour straight ahead, and as if we were shot from a cannon. The nose went straight up. The airplane shook. We all screamed and the left wing, by the hand of God, left the hole it had carved in the ground. We shuddered and we limped back into the sky through the fog again.

John asked the pilot, "Can't we just go on to Chicago? Do we have to land here?"

"We have already diverted from Pittsburgh."

We were in trouble. The bells rang. The red lights blinked. We started to dump fuel. There was nowhere to go except down.

A brave pilot dumped fuel, prayed—went down again—landed on the runway in Erie in a closed airport—stopped the plane—got off. There was a piece of the left end of the wing about two feet wide and one-and-one-half feet long hanging from the end of that wing. All the rivets were broken off the wings. My family, the Carter Family, lived to sing "Will the Circle be Unbroken" again.

Larry Gatlin and his brothers and sister got home safely after their very first show with us.

Carl Perkins lived to play "Blue Suede Shoes" again. The Tennessee Three could play that famous boom-chicka-boom for Johnny while he sang "I Walk the Line" another time. Our family and friends all got off that airplane in the fog.

I chartered a Greyhound Bus—seventeen hours to Nashville. Nineteen people rode with me.

The next week John and I ran into Kris Kristofferson in the airport in New York.

"Kris, you're a pilot. What do you think about a DC9 that accidentally landed in a field, broke off the left end of the wing—nose went every way but upside down, then up in the sky. Shudder-shudder-shudder."

"You wouldn't live to talk about it. You wouldn't have a chance."

We had one.

We took it.

We made it. . . .

I forgot we're on stage, honey.

A VIEW OF THE BRIDGE FROM THE SIDE OF THE ROAD

Prayer is just a conversation with God. One-sided, since I'm usually asking more than thanking, and hardly ever listening. God spoke to me when I was rushing to John's hospital bed, and for once I listened.

I can see the approach to the bridge pretty good. Way down the bank I can hear the sounds of the barges and boats as they move up and down the Cumberland River. There is a long aluminum railing blocking my view from where I lie in the gravel. I am just beside the road that leads to I-40E and I-40W. To the left I can see parts of the traffic cutting to the left of Nashville, Tennessee, going south on I-65. I have been here for quite a while. The cars speed by me very fast. I see the wheels of the eighteen-wheelers—the vans—the buses. They've gone by for days now. If I were alive I could raise my head a little higher and see just across the bridge down in the flats by the river, the multimillion-dollar complex of Nashville Metro near the river. I think I must have been thrown from a car. What I don't understand is why the guardrail did not cut off an arm or a leg. I think my shoes are gone. I seem to be somewhere out of my body now, watching this same scene as the cars move within six or eight feet of my feet. They speed by. They look straight ahead. They do not look down.

Can no one see my legs? They are clearly visible, even from a driver's point of view. Surely somebody will stop any minute—any hour—any day. But then they don't. They just speed by, and I lie here with the hide flayed off my body from scooting in the gravel. How did I get over that rail, or under it. I don't know—for I am dead.

Will my flesh finally, after two days and nights, start to stink and draw the buzzards to my plight? Will no human come to find me and at least tell my family that I am dead? Will I go back to dust and dirt, and only the bones be a reminder to the world that I once had a living soul as they have now? I am somewhere between life and death, hovering over a lifeless body and the busy world that goes to and from work, the trucks that haul produce and product, the police cars that patrol, the buses that carry school children; I see you all so well. Do you not know me? Will you never see these torn and bleeding legs, or notice the blood on the guardrail? Will you never care? God, do you care? I am asking you for help.

Someone else is out there this morning asking for help. I know it. It is a meeting of our souls, beseeching God to care. She is driving near me now, praying as I. Her prayer is for life. I can feel it. She asks you, God, to let her husband live. He's lost so much blood because of a bleeding ulcer. He, too, bleeds as I did. She turns her head to the right—or did you turn it for her, God? I can feel it. I know. She has seen the blood. She has also seen my feet. She has jammed on her brakes. There are many cars—honking their horns at her. She moves slowly on toward the bridge—caught up in the traffic that will not let her stop to see. But she knows that I lay here by the side of the road.

That was June Carter Cash who went on to Baptist Hospital, where her husband, Johnny Cash, clings to life by a thread. They've given him twenty-one units of blood by now. He has survived his surgery.

She has called the police. "Please—some girl is lying by the side of the road bloody. There is no movement."

"Yes, Mrs. Cash. We've got a car there now. The girl is dead. She looks as if she's been there a while."

Maybe ten thousand vehicles passed within six feet of the dead girl. Her name was JANE DOE.

"Someone probably threw her from a car. We think that she has been murdered. She's been there probably two days and nights."

I sat beside John in the hospital and thanked God for his life. I thanked God for the force that met my prayer somewhere near that Cumberland River Bridge and made me turn my eyes to the empty body that lay beside the road, and I thanked God for the living soul of John; and the soul of JANE DOE embraced mine for a minute and went on to stand in final judgment before God.

Mollie Carter Cash—the $5,000 coon hound.

DOG HAIRS

I am embarrassed to admit that my husband and son own a $5,000 dog. I know the world is crazy, but for $5,000 I would expect a dog to sing, dance, and tell funny stories. All this one does is love my son as much as I do. Maybe she's worth it.

I hate dog hairs. Dog hair knows it. It leaves the pores of a dog, floats, sticks, or lies on couches—somewhere near me. I am a walking magnet for "dog hair."

My good friend, Dixie Dean Hall, is a dog nut. She raises and shows bassett hounds. She organizes charity shows for dog hair. She is almost a foster sister to Helen, Anita, and I, having lived with my mother Maybelle and father Ezra. Momma introduced her to Tom T. Hall, so he became a member of the singing family of Cashes and Carters and holds his head up, stands by Dixie and her dogs, and sings his story-telling songs. He also likes dog hair.

Dixie, don't ever give me a dog. I hate dog hair. But then Dixie (having a true love for dogs, on which hair grows), being so close to the family, gives John Carter Cash a dog. What else—not just any dog. Mollie Carter Cash by name—often referred to by me as that blamed $5,000 black-and-tan out-of-the-Oregon-State-Champion big dog. This is a coon dog.

Coon dogs go to the farm with their little boy and his father, get out late at night with friends from Hickman County, Tennessee, and run full force, yelling and howling, a few barks now and then, after the coons. They pick up the trail and away they go after the coon. They stop only when the coon, tired and angry, climbs up the tallest tree for protection.

The little boy, daddy, and friends build a fire, and sing the best coon-rallying song in Tennessee—while peeing on the fire. It's a part of the ritual of coon hunting.

Now Mollie Carter Cash has been trained to hunt coons. She's followed the little boy all over the farm at home, nose to the ground, trailing the coon skin that J.C.C. has dragged in various paths all over to show her where to grab and clutch after father and friends shake the coon out of the tree, which is preferably a persimmon tree. (Coons love persimmons.)

After a night of coon hunting at Bon Aqua farm, I'm free of dog hair—near the fire in the living room of the old log house—happy and clean—I can hear J.C.C. and Mollie on the front porch.

J.C.C.: Mollie, you're supposed to stay with the other coon dogs hot on the trail of the coon. You're not supposed to wait and walk by my leg.

MOLLIE: *(Don't ever walk by my leg again dog look.)*

J.C.C.: You're not supposed to pee on the fire! We are.

MOLLIE: *(Never pee on the fire again look.)*

J.C.C.: Don't go to sleep while all the other hounds are howling at the coon in the tree.

MOLLIE: *(Never go to sleep while treeing coon again look.)*

J.C.C.: Get out of the way when we're shaking the coon down.

MOLLIE: *(Sure, J.C.C. look.)*

J.C.C.: *(Holding her head in his hands.)* Here, let me see. Did that coon hurt you when you sat on it? I mean, when it bit you after you sat on it? Oh, by the way, Mollie. Go on inside and sit on Momma's lap. Be sure to get dog hair on her. She loves dog hair.

Patsy Cline.

PATSY

I sing, but secretly I don't think I am a singer. There are singers, and Patsy Cline was one. She could take a song and turn a noisy five-thousand-seat auditorium into a cathedral-quiet room. She had heart to match her voice, and we won't forget her.

I had a green-speckled capsule once.

"Patsy, I can't stand this. That horse is dead. I know it is."

That beautiful animal had given the run of his life. He had pulled the little rig, and driver behind it—dashed and raced around that track in Philadelphia, Mississippi, and that wonderful horse had beaten them all. She threw back her head—could not seem to stop—reared in her harness, throwing rig and driver over—went head first and died. Her heart burst. There, in front of all of us. It was Patsy Cline and me that stood sobbing to the side of the fairground stands. That animal had just run the fastest record at the track. Her life was finished. She was young, she was beautiful, she was a winner—and she was dead.

We were trying to go on stage. My mascara was running and streaking my face, and I wasn't very pretty. "I'm sick," I said. "I can't sing." Patsy knew that even if I wasn't sick, I couldn't sing very well. She didn't care. I think she liked me because I couldn't sing. It didn't matter. She could. I always went on first if we worked together. I'd play my banjo, my guitar, my Autoharp, sing Carter family songs, and then I'd tell funny stories. How could I make anyone laugh. I didn't feel very funny.

"My head hurts. I'm not having a good time."

"Shut up and go on," she said. "Here, take this. You'll feel better."

"What is it?" I said.

"It'll stop the pain," she said. "It's a little stronger than an aspirin."

I'd had an aspirin in my life, but that was about all.

That little-stronger-than-an-aspirin green-speckled capsule knew that right away. I swallowed it—it dissolved—went straight into my bloodstream—into the ends of my fingers, the tips of my toes. The ends of my hair curled up and suddenly went straight as a stick. I pole-vaulted out on the stage by way of my guitar neck—I do believe that I never touched the stage at any time that night. Patsy worked—I came back out and we did our duets. I'd never felt better in my life. I still felt better after driving all night back to Nashville. I cleaned house all day—recorded all night—cooked breakfast—mowed the yard—recorded again the next night. My eyes would not close.

"What did you give me, Patsy? My eyes won't close. It's the third day and night and I cannot lie down. I don't want to lie down."

Momma said, "I think Patsy's given you something."

It wasn't something. It was a little green-speckled capsule that kept on going off like a rocket through my very being. By now, I wanted to lay down. I would have swapped places with the horse. My arms and legs were flying, as was my head. I was flying, but Patsy was laughing.

We had laughed a lot together. We were both from Virginia. I was studying in New York City when she won the Arthur Godfrey talent contest. She stayed with me at my home when she first came to Nashville. She cried when Charlie Dick called to tell her he had to go into the service. We talked all night a few times. We shared a lot of secrets. I knew all about her—she knew all about me. Sometimes she'd call late at night and just say, "Pray with me, June." I did that several times.

We were driving in California in a car that I had rented. We were playing clubs all over; we had just left Oxnard, and she was driving.

"I'm going out soon," she said. "You write something down for me."

She'd said this to me before—and I'd always shut her up. This night was different. I wrote down what she said.

"I want my mother to raise my daughter and Charlie to raise my son. Be sure to tell them for me, June. Have them bring me home for my wake. I don't want to stay in a funeral home. I want to be home."

That trip was the last time I saw Patsy alive. It was no surprise when they said she was killed in a plane crash with Randy Hughes, Cowboy Copas, and Hawkshaw Hawkins.

They brought her home. I kept the children when they took her to bury her.

The girl had run the fastest record at the track. Her life was finished; she was young, she was beautiful, and she was dead.

Home.

WEATHER
REPORT

Tornados don't come to Nashville, so any black cloud is just a thunderstorm—good for the crops. If you're curious about what it's like living through one, go see the **Wizard of Oz.** *I don't want to talk about it.*

I think I'll lay here on the stairs for a while. I don't think I can walk. I don't even dare to breathe. There's enough air outside. I can hear it more as an explosion than gentle and kind air. This wind is cruel and hard. Don't cry, little son. It's all right. You're tight against my breast, and nothing is going to hurt you—I don't think.

"Carlene, Rosey, Suzie, get behind the big fireplace. Don't move." What has happened? Where is John? Are we all still alive? Fifteen minutes before we were all very much alive. I was nursing my new baby, John Carter Cash, in our big round bed overlooking a slightly troubled lake. I saw only a small black cloud, and Johnny Cash and I were laughing.

We had a lot to laugh about, as we waited for Carlene, Rosey, and Cousin Suzie to come home from Hendersonville. After six daughters, God had given us a son—little John Carter Cash in my arms. All was quiet. All was happiness. All was well. It sounded just like a whirlwind. Whi-zz, whi-zz, whi-zz. No more than that.

I leaped with my baby in arms outside our bedroom door; fell over his little body. John jumped over me, ran down the stairs, threw open the front door, yanking Suzie, Carlene, and Rosey in at the same time. We heard an explosion, and our house shook. We just lie where we were in shock.

"John, I know the roof is gone. I heard it fly off. Please go look if you dare go outside."

There was so much water and dust, we could not see what had really happened outside. We were all alive and well, if not able to move very fast. John was moving, and fast!!

"Mother, you should have seen it. It came from nowhere, this huge black funnel, and the wind, where did the wind come from—"

"I don't know, Rosey. I don't know, Carlene. I don't know, Suzie."

"The roof's still on the house. What was the explosion? I think we've just had a tornado, June."

"John, please hold John Carter a minute. I'm gonna look out on the lake here. I'll look next door at Brack and Anna's house. Good thing it's so strong. All those huge timbers one hundred fifty feet in the air, under roof now. Thank God.

"John, I can't see Brack's house from here. I've always been able to see it from this window. I can't see anything."

"I can't either."

"What's that floating by? I think Brack lost some of those big timbers. There's some in the water just even with our house.

"How did those big logs get in our cove to the right? They're not ours, are they?"

"I don't know. I'd better go see. Take the baby."

"Momma, I'm scared."

"I'm scared, too."

Five minutes later, John was back.

"I've found Brack's house. You're right, it's not there any more. There's some of it on our roof. Some of it cleared our roof. That's it in our cove there. There is not one log left—not one timber standing."

That massive structure on our cliff above our home is no more. God flattened it to make our tennis court, and he knew Mel Tillie needed some big timbers and couldn't hardly ask for them.

June Carter Cash.

RESTORATIVE

There's no way to explain how Johnny Cash and June Carter Cash got involved in restoring downtown Asbury Park, New Jersey. When I try to explain it, nothing makes sense. It has something to do with giving back some glory to a place that deserves it, but you really have to be there to understand.

I like playing here at the Garden State Arts Center. It's beautiful. The grass, the trees, the amphitheater. It doesn't remind me of New Jersey. I'd seen more of the oil tanks and refineries around the Newark Airport, but this part of New Jersey was after my soul.

Bob Wootton—leader of the band and great boom-chicka-boom sound, that ghost of a Henderson sound with a little more Bob than Luther—our friend and guitar player, said, "I've got a friend coming tonight. He makes guitars. I like him. He might make me a guitar."

"Bring him around. Your friend is our friend." So John and I said hello to Henry and, in my mind's eye, I had visions of him working in his garage, hovered over a workbench, in his spare time, of course, sanding away on Bob Wootton's new guitar. I figured with care, he could finish it in a year.

"I like Bob's friend, Henry."

"I like him, too."

"Hey, out there. That guitar player, Henry, Bob's friend from New Jersey, right?"

"Right."

"Has he finished Bob's guitar yet? He started it over a year ago."

"I don't know."

"Hey, Bob. That guitar player, Henry. Did he ever finish your guitar? He doesn't play guitar. How's he gonna make one, if he can't play one."

"He didn't make it."

"I doubted he would."

"Oh, I've got it."

"You have. Where?"

"That's it I've been playing all year on the stage."

"That guitar? It sure don't look homemade. How'd he get that made in his garage?"

"He didn't make it in the garage."

"Then he ordered it, right."

"No. He made it in the factory."

"The factory?"

"Yeah, the factory where he made all the instruments."

"What 'all the instruments'? All of ours?"

"Yeah, ours. The bass, too."

"I'll bet he doesn't play bass, either."

"Hey, John, look here at this newspaper. Is that Henry? Yeah, the one in the middle is Henry. The one sitting on that big balloon with those other six men clinging to the edges of it. It looks as if it is blowing away."

"Let me see. It's not a balloon, June. It's the roof of the Berkeley Carteret Hotel in Asbury Park, New Jersey. Can you believe that seven men have got the nerve to hold down and ride on a rubber roof that is brand new and literally being raised by a hurricane?"

Hold her, Henry. Don't let her go. Hang onto that roof. We need it. It not only covers the new restoration effort of that grand old hotel, it covers the top of our apartment overlooking the Atlantic Ocean. Be sure John Carter and young Henry aren't on that roof. I hope they're downstairs safe somewhere. Why are we living part-time in the Berkeley Carteret in Asbury Park, New Jersey? Someone said the little town was damaged beyond repair from the riot in the sixties. It sits silent in the ghost of dignity it once knew. The echoes of a grand place and grand time, the walking, the seven miles of boardwalk, the solid copper merry-go-round, the grand buildings trimmed in the old copper that's reached the green gold of color through the years. Deal: New Jersey to the left, Ocean Grove to the right. We spend part of our time there, working with Henry Vaccaro on a project to restore this neighborhood. The old opera house, the convention center. It's becoming alive again. It's getting well again. I look, and we are there again. I work to hold onto the memory of a grand and glorious time.

Within the dream of a good friend, a contractor, builder, I play the part of happiness and hope, as I grow older, I'll be able to preserve me, a person—and think back to the splendor of my youth.

I figured he was serious when he refused to blow away in that hurricane. After all, we could use that roof. It covered our head and two hundred sixty-eight rooms of people with the massive ballrooms and wonderful food, and besides we have two thousand people coming for Sunday brunch.

A man that doesn't have any more sense than to build the largest guitar company in the world, when he can't even play a guitar, doesn't have any more sense than to restore a broken-down neighborhood and hotel to the wonder that it was in the twenties.

HANK TUM

Hank Williams was never one of my babies.
He was too wild, too bent on burning up the
gift he had. Oh, I tried—we all did—moth-
ering, brothering, being there. But he had his
own way to go and he went alone.

Left to right: **Kris Kristofferson, Johnny Cash, Willie Nelson, Hank Williams, Jr., Waylon Jennings.**

H ank, I ought to wear you out.

"How could you? Don't you know that was Anita. That wasn't Audrey. Just because Anita was driving Audrey's car is no sign that you could run her in the ditch. She barely got away from you. You can't take your car and run my daughter off the road time and time again.

"Have something to eat. You've got to eat, Hank, and sleep. If you ever got any sleep, you'd love it. Audrey's not here. She's afraid of you. I'm afraid of you. She's with June. They'll be here in a minute."

"But Momma—Maybelle," he said.

"Please don't 'but Momma' me. I'm June's, Helen's, and Anita's Mom. I'm not your Mom. Sometimes I think I am, though. You children have got to stop this fighting. Please take care of yourself, Hank. It's hard for all of us to work with you if you can't control your love for Audrey any more than you do."

"Love? I hate her," he yelled. But we knew better. Audrey knew better as she hid behind me, and my mother became again the mediator between two people walking a thin line between love and hate—on a collision course to fame, fortune, pain, and death. Mother Maybelle put her little arm around Hank Williams, and he began to get control of himself.

"I'm sorry I almost killed you, Anita. I thought you were Audrey. I'm sorry, Audrey. Let's go home."

"I'm afraid of you, Hank."

"I'm fine now. Really I am. You know I'd never hurt you, would I, June?"

"No. I really don't think you would but Audrey is one of my best friends Hank, and I guess Audrey thinks you will."

"Damn it. I love her," he said.

It was a love with such possession, power, jealousy, and hate that it consumed like a fire. It was burning him alive. We had watched it for a year—the joy of Hank, Jr. (Bocephus), the desire for Audrey, his inability to control his temper, the genius of the man, his songs, his poetry, his addiction to drugs—all pointed to the most frightening conclusion.

"Come home with us, June," he said. "It was just a lover's quarrel. I won't hurt her."

"I'll go with him if you'll come too, June. I can't go without you."

He appeared calm, hugged Momma and Anita. Audrey got in my car, and he followed us to their house.

Audrey and I got out of the car on Franklin Road and walked up on the breezeway toward the side door.

He started to yell at her again.

He promised me he would be all right. I thought he would be, and just like that, I heard the bullet fly by my head. It lodged in the side of the house not two feet from my head.

"Hank, how could you?" I screamed.

"I thought you were Audrey," he said. He really didn't mean to fire the pistol at me.

Ashamed, he got in his car and drove away.

Audrey and I cried all night.

I married Carl Smith. Audrey left Hank. I was happy. Hank and Audrey were miserable. He'd talk of nothing but her. The love-hate songs would pour out of him.

Carl, Hank, and I were at a baseball game.

"That's Audrey," he said. "I know it is."

He could always see her somewhere.

Anita was getting married.

"Let me talk to Audrey, June. I'm getting married, too," he said. "I wish it was Audrey."

"Hello, Hank. It's too late." And she hung up.

I'll never really know, but I think he thought his bride was Audrey.

Thirty some years later—life, births, and deaths have passed us by.

He lay on a pillow with his head split open, wired and put back together—not quite straight, but with a prayer, after many operations, Hank Jr.'s face would be straight again. I held his hand and prayed while holding Audrey's hand in my other one. I thanked God that Hank Jr. would live after falling off that five-hundred-foot mountain in Missoula, Montana. John stood at the foot of his bed. Bocephus mumbled a greeting to us. "You look awful," he said.

I thought we'd never get here. It's a long ways. Don't you dare die. Your daddy beat you to it years ago.

John said, "You might as well kiss that eye good-bye, Bocephus," and Bocephus started to laugh from the depths of the Valley of Death.

Audrey said, "Oh, Lord, I thought you were Hank."

Hank Williams died somewhere between Knoxville, Tennessee, and Oak Hill, West Virginia. It was 1953, New Year's Day. We were in Charleston, West Virginia, just sixty miles from him when they found him crumpled in the back seat of a car. We would never be able to stand him up and help him walk again. We loved him, we had lost him, and we still miss him.

Johnny and Elvis.

HOPE AND ELVIS PRESLEY

Elvis was just making it when we met; he'd bought his first Cadillac, and none of us knew then how many Cadillacs, how many miles his path would take. You would have liked this Elvis—old stick in the mud.

They call it black gumbo. It has a smell all of its own. Most flatland cotton pickers from Arkansas love it. It's rich in all the minerals that encourage cotton to push its way out of the ground and burst into a brand new pod of cotton on its way to my back by way of a dress, or to cover my body in a cool, cool sheet. I love cotton.

Watermelons love black gumbo. They spring from this gooey substance in the hot, dry air of the Arkansas mornings and develop into the largest watermelons in the world. You hope for a sweet-tasting red melon that only comes from that word hope. You hope its yours—and to be better than all the rest, too, to be a watermelon from Hope, Arkansas.

"I hope it doesn't rain too hard."

"It's a shortcut," Elvis cried.

He was in front of us. His first new pink Cadillac, Scotty and Bill, Red West, Justin Tubb, Pete Wade, and Jimmy Snow—were all enjoying screaming at us out the windows of this new, almost not used, two shades of pink Cadillac. It was a powerful engine, shiny and new looking—it made those men feel wonderful. We were dragging the Arkansas highways, singing "Cry, Cry, Cry."

We were the Carter Girls, Anita, myself, Becky Bowman (sitting in for Helen), and Mother Maybelle. We were the ones in the red-and-white Cadillac limousine. It was a fun day. Dragging, yelling from car to car. Having fun, hoping for a shortcut to Hope, Arkansas. We were all first in one car, then the other.

"I think that road's too wet, Elvis!"

But he turned left. What appeared to be his eight-mile shortcut was a sea of mud. We were both driving so fast that, by the time I had been able to stop, I had made the same stupid left turn, and we had glided about one-half mile into the Arkansas gumbo before my wheels caught the dirt and gravel. His beautiful new car was up to the axle, being pulled down like a magnet further and further into the mud.

"I'll push you."

Scotty and Bill jump out. Red brings his support system (muscles), flashes us a smile, and pushes. We girls stay in the strong old Cadil-

lac, where it's secure, and attempt to push him with our front
bumper. The wheels spin.

"Push him out, Red."

Red West is a football player.

"Hey, push us, too, Red. Help."

Our wheels spin, and we laugh at the guys. Now Pete, Jimmy, and
Justin are also up to their knees in mud pushing.

"Becky, you get out and push."

"What?"

"Yeah, you with the long-billed cap, with the wet washcloth dripping in your eyes. You're cool. You get out."

"I play accordion, bass, and guitar. I do not push cars."

"They're all getting too hot out there. You're bigger than we are.
You're stronger. They might need you to wring out our ice cold
washcloth over one of their heads."

"Oh, sure. Why doesn't Elvis get out? I could drive his pink Cadillac."

"He might get his new saddle shoes dirty."

"Oh."

"Maybe we should turn around."

"How? We're stuck now, going straight ahead."

"Thank God, we're going straight ahead. Let's hope we don't continue to go straight down."

"His car won't budge."

"Let's back up."

"How?"

I know now how Arkansas does it. The dirt that should be dirt is
not dirt at all. It's gloop that sucks you down into the mire, covers
one pink Elvis car and one red-faced Elvis (mad, too, I might add).

"Quit laughing, you silly girls."

"You want me to cry, Momma. It's your fault, Elvis!! It's definitely
not mine. Why'd you turn left anyway?"

"I was in a hurry," and, like all the girls in America, we must have
been, too. We darted off into this same mud hole.

"I hate you, Elvis Presley. We're gonna miss our radio interview."

"We're stuck, too."

"Leave him alone, June."

"I'm doing that all right, Momma. I'm leaving him alone in that car. He's leaving me alone in this car. This mud is going to drag us down. Oh, thank the Lord, there's a truck. A wonderful left-turning green pickup truck. That's all right, Momma."

"Help—Help. It's me and Elvis and Momma and the girls."

"Help—help."

"You all stuck?" asked the good ole farmer boy.

"Yeah, could you give us a push?"

"I'll try. Can't push these girls. They can't move for you in the pink Cadillac. I got a rope. I'll see if I can get around you both."

"Watch it! Watch it!"

"We'll get back in the car with you, Elvis."

"You boys aren't getting in my new car with all that mud on you."

"You can't get in ours, either. Oh, there went that pretty little green left-turning pickup truck in the ditch."

"In a more muddy ditch, you mean. Scotty, Bill. Get out, get up, and crawl in the back of that truck, put some weight in it. Maybe the wheels will take hold. Help! Help!"

"Girls first," said the good ole country boy, flashing us a smile.

"That's a puny-looking rope there. See if you can hook it on the front bumper—down there under the gumbo. Dig. You'll find it, Scotty. Oh good. There goes Elvis. Hurrah, Hurrah. Maybe we can turn around after this little curve."

"We can't if we can't find a drive. There's six-foot ditches on both sides of this road."

"What are you stopping for?"

"I'm stopping to quit pulling this pink Cadillac. I'm going back to push the girls a little ways," said the little green truck driver.

"What?" asked Elvis.

"Yeah, what." (A don't-care look from the driver.)

"My new car."

"Looks like theirs is a little newer than yours. Hang on to the back, boys. All right, you pretty girls, give her the gas. Here we go."

"Yeah, here we go. How about that? We're moving—just like a bullet through the glue. Watch out, Elvis. Here we come."

"My bumper," said Elvis.

"Look, I don't like it back here behind your bumper. There's no-where else to go. Go back up there and pull poor old Elvis again. It's his first car. He loves it."

"It's my first life, Momma. I love it."

Good ole country boy, with Scotty, Bill, Jimmy, Justin, and Pete in the back of the truck, also bewildered Red West with lots of mud, pull Elvis with rope—leave him stuck—rev engine—slide sideways—almost lose boys—run back and push girls—listen to Elvis holler. Pay no attention. Smile at girls. Push girls to Elvis's bumper. Rev good old motor on left-turning green pickup truck and go fasten rope on Elvis's front bumper again. Over and over and over. One hundred feet at a time. I know that mud road drove Jimmy Snow to preach the gospel, Scotty Moore and Pete Wade to produce records, Justin Tubb to write, Becky Bowman to go home to St. Jo and raise kids, and Red West to develop new muscles.

"It's your fault, Elvis."

"It is not my fault, June."

"Do you know what's going to happen to us, Elvis? This Arkansas mud has a plan. I know now how they do it. All these minerals, I mean."

After three hours.

It would have happened again, if it hadn't been for a good old boy in a left-turning green pickup truck who pushed and pulled us inch by inch for eight miles. We would literally have been sucked into the Arkansas gumbo—digested by some unknown good thing—and finally June Carter, her mom, and the Carter girls could have ended up a boll of cotton, and Elvis Presley could have been the biggest watermelon in the world.

The Carter sisters.

EARLY MORNING NASHVILLE WSM RADIO

We were show business, but we didn't know it. All we Carter girls knew was getting up in the dark, showing up at the radio station, singing with sleep still in our eyes, and starting the real day right after. Didn't everybody do that?

She doesn't have on her hose yet. "We're late. We'll never make it. Helen, you could make one radio program without your nylon stockings and high heel shoes on. Leave them under the bed. Stand up, Anita. Better still, wake up. Then why should you wake up? You've been doing these early-morning radio shows for five years and you've slept through them all.

"Breakfast is ready."

"I'll have two eggs, some of those good biscuits, and gravy, Momma, and some crisp bacon. Did we eat all the country ham yesterday morning? I just got one piece. If you wouldn't feed all the young men on the Grand Ole Opry every morning, there'd be a lot more for me to eat. Helen's taking her hair down. Why does she always do that? She should just pull it back in a pony tail and pray for it. That's what I do."

"Hold still, Anita. Put this dress on. I'll button it up. Wait a minute, I'll roll up your pajama legs. Don't jump up and down when we get to the studio. Just sing high and play your bass fiddle. Yesterday morning, you got to pattin' your foot, and your pajama leg fell down under your dress on "Keep on the Sunny Side." Let go of the bedpost. Leave the pillow here.

"Bring me another biscuit and honey, Momma. I'll eat it while I drive.

"Yeah, Helen, your hair looks all right. Yeah, your lipstick is the right color. Try walking, Anita. You're too heavy for me to carry. One foot in front of the other. Hut–2–3–4. This way, out the door.

"Momma, you sit in the back seat and tune my Autoharp. I can't drive, hold Anita, and eat my biscuit all at the same time. Anita, rest your head on the left side of the bass fiddle neck. We ought to put her big old classic bass back up on top of the car. The cover matches our little trailer we pull in the back. The pegs on the head keep jamming into my right ear.

"Helen, why are you putting on mascara at five o'clock in the morning?

"I don't care if it is the National Life and Accident Insurance Company Building. We'll be lucky if we see anyone except the announcer, Jud Collins, the engineer Charlie Bragg, and the janitor. They don't care about mascara.

"Watch for cops."

"I can't slow down. We've got to tune when we get there."

"You're not going to make it."

"I'll make it if you do. There—I'll park right here where it says president—*National Life and Accident Insurance Company—No Parking.* Anita, get your nose out from between your bass strings. We've got to get this dude upstairs. I'll carry the bass, or better still, I guess, I'll do it like I always do.

"Anita, you carry the bass—I'll carry you. Don't wake up now, please. You don't know you can't lift the bass, and the shock of finding yourself carrying it might make you drop it.

"Momma, have you got my Autoharp and your guitar? Where's Helen?"

"She went upstairs with her makeup case."

"Where's Chester? Old Chet will surely come back down and bring up Helen's forty-pound accordion. He'll do that for her. I'll get her to ask him. He won't do that for me—I just broke his D'Angelico guitar yesterday. He'll probably never speak to me again. I dreamed he beat me to death with the neck that was left from his guitar. Both pieces still looked pretty good to me when I was running. Where's my Autoharp pick? I've got honey on my fingers from the biscuit and honey. No, Chester, I didn't bring you a biscuit.

"Helen, fit your accordion into the grooves in your stomach. Anita, hang on to the bass fiddle neck—do not fall slowly to the floor. Stand up to the right of the microphone. I'll punch you with my foot when it's time for you to sing. Just open your mouth. The tenor part will come out like it always does.

"Helen, quit spraying all that perfume on yourself. I'm allergic to it. I'll be sneezing on "Will the Circle be Unbroken."

"Hi, Chester. I'll just stay over here.

"There goes the red light. Momma—Momma.

"Please flash a tragic look at everybody. We're on the air."

"Now you bake right, with Martha White
Goodness Gracious, good and light
Martha White."

Front gate of the Cinnamon Hill Great House.

RANSOM

I have never in my life been more truly fright-ened. Being scared didn't surprise me, being angry did. For I was angry at these men who came into my house, threatened those I loved most, and wanted to steal or break things that were rightfully mine. The fear faded, but the anger is still there.

I could almost see my face. The eyes, the nose, the chin flickered in light waves as the candlelight bade them come and go. The long, dangling earrings flashed a bit of gold, pure and pink with bits of diamonds, rubies, sapphires, and turquoise here and there. These were my very favorites. The image was vague.

You can't see very well, looking into the solid dark brown mahogany floors. They shine like glass, though. Isn't that nice? I love the strength of dark Jamaican mahogany, on the staircase, on the massive doors, on the window shutters and sills—but I must remember to thank Miss Dessna, Miss Victoria, for the care they give this wonderful wood, and Miss Edith, too. Sure, I'll do that. I like Ray Fremmer's tile on his great house floor. It's Minton, and early Minton. Good for him and his dining room. I could see him pretty good from where I lay on the floor. He was lying between Doug (John Carter's friend) and John on our dining room floor—at our Cinnamon Hill Great House in Jamaica. I'm so glad Ray doesn't have his gun with him tonight. Thank you, God, that he left it at Green Park in all the building and construction going on there. Thank God for the gun law in Jamaica that sends you to prison for life for illegally carrying a gun. Chuck did not have a gun—but, most of all, I was thankful that John did not have a gun with him. He is a quiet and gentle man, but he is a terror beyond words when he is mad. A gun in his belt would have definitely been a mistake that day of our lives—a big mistake. Guns kill people.

My head was near Reba's at the head of the table on the Caribbean side. Her chin quivered, my chin quivered, and we exchanged glances, aware that her husband, between she and John, felt compelled to do something—anything. After all, he was security, wasn't he? But, most of all, Reba and I knew that, if we were to survive this night, we would have to pray to God that Johnny Cash would control himself. We were probably more frightened that he might not be able to be still. It was hard to be still.

"Do not look up, mon! Keep your face down on the floor. All of you—down."

The words were muffled in a country Jamaican dialect—sifted by the stocking covering his face. Features are lost under stocking faces—but one thing I could see was the gun in his hand. He held it to Doug's head and screamed. "We want two million dollars in five minutes or this boy is dead!!"

Did this stocking-faced man not know about the gun law? It didn't seem to matter. They came through the living room just like that.

I wonder what God thought? For we were all talking to God. Miss Edith (our cook), Miss Dessna and Miss Victoria (our maids) were singing the blessing. Our heads were all bowed. We gave thanks— for the Christmas that was good and the joys of love and life.

One carried a hatchet, one a knife, and then that rusty-looking gun. Would it fire?

You don't know—you don't care. The combination has the power of a possible nuclear attack.

"You can have all our money. You can have anything you want. Don't hurt the children. Don't do something you'll be sorry for," John said.

"This isn't the right little boy," one screamed to the other. Hatchet said, "You've got the wrong boy!!"

Big Hat–Big Gun grabbed John Carter by the hair, pulled him up off the floor by his father, and there it is again. Only this time the pain in your chest is worse, because it's your son—it was horrible even when it was someone else's son, but now it was mine. I could not breathe. I pleaded with my eyes under the table to John. Please don't move—give them what they want.

Big Hat–Big Gun screamed, "Search them all, mon."

"We're hungry, mon."

"We want your money, mon."

"I'll shoot you, mon."

There are only three bad people in all of Jamaica, I thought. Why are they all here? Why us? Why have they come? My son, my son. Hatchet stood at the head of the table on the mountain side, and Sharp Knife searched us all. I watched under the table as we all lay still on the floor, Big Hat–Big Gun sticking that gun everywhere, even in John Carter's ear.

There is nothing like watching a stocking-faced thing with knife in hand, groping his way, searching you for any money or jewelry, any-thing on your person that he might grab and clutch for his very own. He moves like a growing fungus, closer and closer until you know your time is near. How does anyone have the right to defile you as a person? How dare he think he can put his hand on you, searching or otherwise? But then, they are the machines; you are the victim.

There stands my son. He says a straightforward "Yes, sir." He answers loud and clear, "Yes, sir." He does not move. He is very brave. The gun is still at his head.

John flashes me a keep-your-head signal.

I try.

I'm scared.

Miss Edith has high blood pressure. Miss Vicki is crying, Miss Dessna is quiet. Ray Fremmer is quiet and unpredictable. John is furious but has enough sense to fear for our lives. Reba's husband is following John's lead to play a waiting game. Reba is frightened but under control.

I'm scared to death. My face is on the floor. My husband might kill somebody. We might try to help him. Ray Fremmer just could have that gun somewhere, and, as they search, then he could kill one of them, or worse yet, get some of us killed. Doug is quiet but has tears on his face. John Carter's just staring straight ahead. Old Sharp Knife is crawling over bodies on the floor, nearer and nearer to me. I'm having a hard time breathing. How could they? How dare they?

I look at my solid gold Geneva watch with the mother-of-pearl face. I look at my emerald and diamond ring. I don't want them to have my favorite ring that John bought me in Israel. There's a big china cabinet just there by my head, and a good-sized leg holding it up. There—just like that—I slip my ring and watch behind that leg on that china cabinet. Let him grab and clutch on that and see if he can find it, I think. Ha.

Oh Lord, what have I done? I'm stupid. What if he saw those pieces as he made us lie on the floor. He could really get mad. The gun was at John Carter's head. All he had to do was pull the trigger. Guns can kill. Oh, Lord, help us all.

He crawls near, half smiling, forceful, mean, with both hands full. My gold chain and my earrings join John's brand new watch. Money and more jewelry. There is no way this paper can receive the truth as to how it makes you feel to be thoroughly searched. You're left with nothing but the bruises on your body and the defiling of your soul and spirit to remind you.

Five minutes are over, and we are still alive. That's good. Maybe they won't kill us.

Crazy Big Hat–Big Gun will now settle for a million dollars.

"They won't let us bring that kind of money on the island," John tells them. "We just don't have that kind of money here. They only allow you $500 in U.S. cash."

"One by one, mon. Take them to their rooms, mon!"

They have our money, they have our jewelry, except watch and ring under the china cabinet. Oh, what'd I do that for? "They'll go now, right?"

"Right." John's eyes say maybe.

"Miss Edith is dying," says Miss Dessna.

She has high blood pressure. She could die.

Big Hat–Big Gun and Crazy, "Let her die, look—"

I've got to sit up. I can't breathe. I gasp.

Big Hatchet at head of table, "Take her first."

Why can't I keep my mouth shut? "You promise me you won't hurt my son. I'll go."

Hatchet's hurt. Hatchets can kill. Big Hat–Big Gun says, "I like your little boy."

"Thank you, sir."

Why didn't I cut my long hair off, I ask. It's too good a handle for people. Sharp Knife pulls the hair with one hand, holds a knife to my throat with the other. My legs fly all by themselves. I run up the stairs because the Knife tells me to. Knives can kill.

My head hurts. I'm glad he let go of my hair. One by one all the drawers are on the floor. He pulls off the mattress from the bed. You walk over all the clothes on the floor. Keep remembering: Don't scream. They'll go now. You give him more money, your mother's diamond earrings, all you have. Do as he says. Oh, my son. The bruises aren't too bad. You hold your head just right so the knife doesn't cut into your neck.

Big Hat–Big Gun screams, "Give us more money, mon, or somebody's gonna die."

Miss Dessna and Miss Vicki, "Miss Edith is really sick."

Sharp Knife. (You're downstairs now because next is next.)

Next.

Next.

Next.

Like a walking nightmare, next and next. They get up off the floor, go to the rooms where they sleep, one by one. They go—the noise—the terror—the scuffle.

My head hurts. "I've got to sit up. Please, can I sit up? I have heart trouble."

Hatchet, "Can she, mon?"

"I won't look at you too closely."

Big Hat–Big Gun, "Somebody's gonna die here tonight if we don't get what we want. I like you, you little redheaded boy."

John Carter, "Thank you, sir."

Big Hat–Big Gun, "This is a real gun."

"I know it is."

"Crazy Big Hat–Big Gun takes John Carter and leaves the room. Noises—trashing rooms, broken furniture, all clothes on floor.

To Hatchet Head, at head of table, "You know you aren't a murderer. I'm afraid of Big Hat–Big Gun. He's building toward killing someone. What if Miss Edith dies?"

Hatchet, "She won't die."

"She could. I could. I have heart trouble."

"Shut up."

I go back to my shut-up position.

"You have all our money. You've torn the house to pieces. My wife does truly have heart trouble, and Miss Edith is a pale gray color. What else do you want of us? Please go," says John.

"Shut up," answers Hatchet.

Sharp Knife, "One, two, three, four bags full. Money, jewelry."

Oh, John, I don't think he'll hurt John Carter. He seems to like him. I try to reassure myself.

More noises.

John comes up off the floor.

Hatchet, "Get down."

Big Hat–Big Gun, "How do you like my new hat?"

In and out, up and down the stairs dragging my little boy. My husband is ready to kill someone with his bare hands.

Hatchet, "C'mon, mon. We've got everything. Let's go."

Sharp Knife, "No, we ain't got it all, mon!!!"

I can't breathe. "Please don't hurt my son. Promise me, dear Hatchet Man. You don't want to kill anyone."

Hatchet, "Shut up."

Get it over with.

One—two hours. Has it really been that long? I'm acting as if I can't breathe, but, from my vantage point of being allowed to sit up in my pleading-dog position, I see that Miss Edith really can't breathe at all.

"Dear Hatchet Man, she's really gonna die, you know. Then they'll get you all for murder."

Hatchet Man, "Come on, mon!!"

Crazy man—Big Gun in another hat outfit in the hall, throwing things and dragging little son back into the dining room. "Come on, woman. Let's see what you have."

Thank God, John. He's let go of John Carter for a while. Now we start to worry about sister Reba. Big Gun is thinking about our sister Reba, too.

Lots of noises—screaming—pushing—yelling—wonder—worry —what to do.

If you move, he kills her or me or him or us all. Please. That man's psychotic, he's crazy. He's gonna kill somebody. Do something, dear Hatchet Man. That time was short but horrible.

I'm going to play the best scene of my life. (Shades of dramatic teacher, Sandy Meisner.) Help me remember how to have a real heart attack.

Signal John, Reba, and Chuck that I'm really all right. Having had something near enough once or twice in my life to a heart attack, I try desperately hard to smile at John Carter, back on the floor now.

Dear Hatchet Man, please let us go. He's crazy. Help us. Close to three hours now. You have everything. One last look at John, Chuck, and Ray, ready for anything now. I can't breathe, Hatchet Man, Sharp Knife. Help me. Dive for the mahogany. Gasp for air. Tremble. Turn blue. Go out like a light.

Reba, "She's had a heart attack. Help us."

John, "Make that Crazy Man go. She could die. I'm not kidding you."

Hatchet Man, "Hey, mon. Come on. This woman's sick. I got two sick women."

Gasp. Gasp.

White look, blue look. Dark blue look.

Sharp Knife, "She really having a heart attack?"

Hatchet Man, "I don't know, mon."

I hear them close to my head. I feel the Hatchet Man hit my head twice. Not hard. Scraped across my hair to the scalp. No hard pain. No blood. Just enough to see if I would move or not.

I did not move. I was quiet. I did not breathe. I begged my heart to cease a minute or two.

Hatchet Man, "Hey, mon. C'mon now. This woman's dying now. Come on."

I still do not breathe. I feel pain now. I am frightened. I am tired. I am sick. I don't remember how they get me down the steps of our basement. I remember being dragged, pulled along the floor—people helping each other up—pushed down those grand ole steps into that basement—into the dungeon. I could have walked, I don't know. The walls were three feet thick with bars on all the ground-level windows, the solid cement floor, that great room of nothing. They hurdle us into that room and we hear the double doors lock behind us.

We hear noises above in the house. Running, screaming, throwing more things.

We are all there, sitting on the cold floor, locked in our own dungeon. We hear noises on the stairs again. I remember to fall back into my heart attack position. Miss Edith sits on the floor surrounded and held in Miss Vicki's and Miss Dessna's arms. The lock clicks, the door opens, and one by one.

Hatchet Man, "Here's some iced tea. You might get thirsty."

Careful not to break the pitcher.

Sharp Knife places turkey and dressing—that wonderful different dressing of Miss Edith's—beautiful trusses on the legs of that turkey—a way of beauty with a bird taught to Miss Edith by some fine French chef off a ship of hope—and three Waterford crystal glasses on a big silver tray.

Crazy Big Hat–Big Gun, "I'm sorry we had to rob you, but we were hungry. We didn't want to take anything from you, the staff, I mean. You may be here a while. Don't scream, don't try to get out. Stay here for at least the night before you make a noise." These doors were two to three inches thick—hard-core mahogany.

We sat within our prison, on the floor. Ray Fremmer took a turkey leg—three hours cold now—and ate it. Someone gave Miss Edith some iced tea. I held John Carter and Doug in each arm. Reba was brave—and blue. John and Chuck found a solid mahogany hat hanger and rack. It served as a battering ram—upstairs we heard noises.

We were afraid again.

I heard a car drive away. I heard the pitter-patter on the floor. "The dogs," John said. "They've put the dogs inside."

We broke and battered the door down in fifteen or twenty minutes and went upstairs. The dogs, our vicious dogs, I might add, wagged their tails for us. The phones were dead. They had taken my Rover car with them. Why did our dogs not attack? I don't know.

There was no place to walk that had not been trashed, except the dining room floor where we were forced to lie. The table still held the roast pork shoulder, the yams, the salads, the fine china with the silver, the Baccarat and the Waterford crystal. The candles burned to the little nothing holes of black deep in the hurricane lamps.

Each of us that was forced to lie on that floor that night have probably very different memories of the special words that were said to us, for we each had to face it, one at a time, in our own way. They had dropped a purse of mine near the Rover car while running. This bag had money and jewelry found in our driveway. The police found my car in Barrett Town, about three miles away, in the middle of the road, with four doors open and a busted oil pan.

There were arrests; some money was heard about. Some may have been guilty. Some were not. It's hard to identify someone with a stocking over his face or a scarf over one-half his face. I hear that one was dead in another robbery attempt, another one was shot and killed, and that one is still at large.

We are all alive and well. I thank God for that. I still live in Jamaica part-time and have been there many times since that

Christmas. We will continue to do so. If John and John Carter go, I will follow them.

Ten or twelve years ago, sister-in-law Reba and I were buying lots of Klediments for our house at Cinnamon Hill—in that wonder-world paradise of Jamaica. We had lots of things in our good friend John Rollins's house, number 17, inside his compound, safe and sound with guards and dogs and such. We were preparing our home there for life, love, and the pursuit of happiness under his care at Copperwood.

The news came from near Ridgetop, Tennessee.

The robbery. The terror. The murder. The murders.

We called him String Bean. He was brave. He played the banjo on the Grand Ole Opry and he was a friend of mine. He liked to fish. Estelle (his wife) drove him to and fro. He wore his overalls with lots of money in the front chest pouch between his galluses. He smiled—saluted you if he loved you, and rode on to a quiet retreat where they lived near the ridge and his good friends, Grandpa and Ramona Jones. He stood lots of times on that Grand Ole Opry stage with his pants—one foot high—shirt maybe three feet high—smiling and picking his banjo and adoring the world.

He must have fought them, they said. There appeared to be a struggle. They shot and killed him. His money was gone. Estelle ran. They shot and killed her in the front yard. "Stay there, June," John said by phone. "It's safer."

Two precious people dead in Tennessee. "I'm sorry," I said. "It's nice to be in Jamaica."

So where does it come from?

I don't know.

Years later, as I polished my emerald ring and gold watch: I wasn't brave on that Christmas. I did stupid things. I could have been like Estelle, laying in the yard with a bullet in the back. I talked too much.

My husband was smarter than most, for we are still alive in Tennessee, and it's like I said. I love Jamaica.

There's only three bad people in that whole God-fearing country by the sea. I just hate that they decided to pay us a visit on that Christmas holiday.

I could not believe that a prime minister, Seaga by name, a man of much importance, cared as much as he did over our hard time. The people by the side of the road took off their hats. My friend, Evelyn Buddle, cried in the night. They waved good-bye to us at the airport, fearing we'd never return.

But we always will.

That country is a country with compassion. My staff has great and glorious love. They really care about us, and we wear our Mickey Mouse watches, carry no money, and cling to the good times there in the trade winds from the Caribbean Sea. For the murderers of String Bean and Estelle still walk around alive in the halls of buildings and in fields and farms near our Tennessee lakeside home.

June with Nancy and Ronald Reagan.

BLINKING EYES

There was real splendor in the Statue of Liberty celebration, and it was real and spontaneous. But one woman's recollection said and meant more than a bargeful of fireworks.

Her nose is over four feet high, and there's spines upon her head, pointed at the end and wider where they join the brain that thinks the things she said.

Somewhere way up high, three hundred and eighty feet, near low clouds and birds and sun—the rain will wash her clean and make her shine, and make you feel as if your life had just begun.

She reaches for a power, as if she hands it up to God for feet to feel at home on streets and land, on places they have never trod. But what wonder that it is, as she lifts her light above the town.

Oh, New York harbor, how you shine as rockets glare into the night and love abounds, for millions line the shore, and billions watch from around the world, and people scream for more. Red, white, and blue explodes two hundred feet of glare and falling fire for me to see.

John, Rosemary, Kate, Karen, and Lou—tears falling in our huddle, as ashes of joy settle in on me. John Denver, Barry Manilow, Whitney Houston, Melissa Manchester, Joel Grey, and James Whitmore brighten to the sound of the Boston Pops with John Williams at the top.

We sway to the sounds, and we are one, as the marching music weaves its magic. It's those who fight and scream for war out there, they're lost; and God, that's tragic.

There are billions out there watching; caught in the euphoria as we are, so let the world know that we stand for Liberty and Freedom, and thank you, France, as that copper lady shines our light.

Let us pray and think of love and hope we never have to fight. But fight, we will, if we have to, and I know you know it now—to the far ends of the earth. I hope we've shown you how.

Let's just bind our hearts together in a world of love, prayer, and peace, and seal it.

I'm reaching out to all of you, Oh, God—just let them feel it.

—July 4, 1986
New York across the bay—Lady Liberty
to my right—and me in Liberty Park,
New Jersey. What a night!!!

148

"Oh, Miss-a June—it'a made me cry. Mister Cash on the Fourth of July. The Ragged Old Flag from Liberty Park at the celebration of July Fourth at Liberty Weekend in New York. I saw you and Mister Cash's picture in *Newsweek* magazine. You saw the president and the two million people. You know I saw it, Miss-a June. Her, I mean. Real close it was. Me, Flora, Josephine, and Jeannette. They were little, and I couldn't speak-a English. But I dragged them upon deck. I said, "Look-a children, there she is. The light in her hand. We come-a to the new world. Our slow Italian ship inched into the New York Harbor up the Hudson, past that Great Lady. We stood-a on the deck and we cried. Me and the children. I leav-a Italy to come-a to Armando in Nashville. The great Copper Lady hold up her hand, the light shine—and I swear Miss-a June, her eyes just blink-a—like lights go on and off—and I pray God just take me to my husband and I learn-a to speak English, and I work-a hard and God to give me somebody to work for that will love me and I be a good woman— and I raise-a my children—and I be a good wife."

This was Anna Bisceglia, my Italian maid, wife of our security chief, Armando. I do know she is an angel unaware. She had been pulled bodily by Armando out of the wreckage of three tragic bombings in Italy, the first, when she was seven years old. This was in World War II, and the scars still line her back in jagged rows. War is bad.

"We had-a nothing to eat, Miss-a June. I was a-scared—once the bombs came, I came to under rocks. Dust, dirt, and the whole building she fall-a down on me. The door, she stand and cover my head. My body don't move—but water drips on my face, and I lift my mouth to sip it—one-a drop at a time. Armando—he find-a me—he save-a me. Three times he save-a me. After the war, he come-a to America for his sister, Anna—she marry Braxton Dixon from American Army. And finally, he send-a for me and the children. Oh, Miss-a June, I was-a so a-scared—by light in Statue of Liberty's eyes. They light up and I happy. I so happy. It is the Promised Land. My family all die except my sister, Josephine, and brother. He is now dead. Thank you, Miss-a June, that Josephine come-a now to America to live. I pray. America is the best-a place in the world.

"God help-a America, and I help-a too, all I can, and Josephine, she help-a, and Armando and Anna [sister-in-law] who marry Braxton who build-a your house. We all help-a. I see Senator Gore at Memphis Roast for Mister Cash. I thank-a him for letter to help-a Josephine. I try to kiss-a his hand. He a nice-a man, Miss-a June."

I know of some of the immigrants—and sometimes when I'm weary and discouraged, I recall the lights of the eyes that Anna could dream to see on the Statue of Liberty. They did not really shine for me. It was the torch that shined for me. But, in her heart, Anna saw them blink on and off and on and off. And I remember her hunger, the living tombs she survived, her love for America, and I sometimes become ashamed that we, in our world of push and shove and trying to matter, cannot stop to have a war fought and the bombs fall on our head and cover us in debris.

The clutter that sometimes covers our lives—and eyes—to the wonderful land that is ours.

For we are all descendants of immigrants—and, better still, some are first immigrants who cry and have visions of the blinking eyes.

They can sometimes see better than we.

MAKING A MEMORY

My men, John and John Carter, have landed me in some strange places. Of course, I didn't have to go along with them, but where's the fun in that? I think maybe I'm just not what you would call an outdoor girl.

John Carter Cash in Alaska.

I believe it's the same things that made our ancestors blaze the trail near Massician Gap, Virginia—through the Wilderness Road, the "Dug Road," the "Old Reedy Creek Road," the road "Down Troublesons," the road through Massician Gap—that made John do it.

"I want to take you somewhere no one has ever been, you and John Carter. Time is flying. Soon our son will be gone. He'll have a girlfriend, and we'll only have the memories of these trips we take to keep us happy in our old age."

"That sounds reasonable."

"Sure, it's reasonable. We'll just fly off to Anchorage, Alaska—take another jet the next day, another hour or hour and a half farther southeast down to the Alaskan port of Dillingham. There he's gonna meet us, Bob Curtis, in his little plane. Then we're going on another hour until we get to the Tikchik Narrows Lodge, a wonderful five-star lodge on the lake in the Land of the Midnight Sun. We'll land there, then our adventure begins."

"Sounds wonderful," I said.

Who alive doesn't think her name should have been Sacajawea at some time in her life. This was going to be great. The clean air, the float trip, the mountains, and the cool of Alaska—on out there where I had never been before.

When Johnny Cash asks another man to do something, he does it, right? Wouldn't you?

We meet good friends, have a wonderful meal, pack our gear into still a smaller plane, and off we fly, over treetops, buzzing caribou, bear, and moose. It's like a Disney film, and John, John Carter, and young, terrible, tumbling, true, and trusted Tim (our guide) were to be the stars.

We reach the top of the Tikchik Narrows River. I know John told me this river had been floated, right John?

Right!

Excitement. Oh, wonder of the fiery sky, over mountain peaks of snow, me and my family with our gear. We're on the mighty <u>GO</u>.

As we land, I see the two rafts, one large enough—about twelve feet—to hold four of us—then the smaller raft—eight feet maybe—will trail behind, floating down gentle rapids for the experience of a lifetime.

I am breathing clear air—gentle and new from the green grass and bushes that lined that snakey river, and we started our float. I feel brand new. The sun has about two hours before setting and it hangs low upon the mountain. I lay down on bags of sleeping bags and gear, and was content. It is quiet, it is good; it is our special time, my son, my husband, and mine.

We must have been floating for an hour and have found a grassy flat place to the right of the river. We pitch our tent—for the three of us—Tim had his own one-man tent, and we have sleeping bags filled with down that we place on inflated rafts as a mattress. This is the way to camp. Tim is a master chef, pulling out the big aluminum box full of gourmet food—great steaks, salad—all the good things to eat. What a wonderful time it is as the sun was setting. The temperature had been about fifty degress and, within five minutes, it has dropped to around freezing. We are ready for it, having brought bags of long handle underwear, waders—clean clothes—just anything you need for the Alaskan Wild—we had it. My teeth are chattering, I have a stocking cap pulled down over my ears, two pairs of socks, rubber boots, and down coats. I can hardly move, but who has to, not me. There is no sound. Nothing. We sing "North to Alaska" and miss Johnny Horton. The wind starts to blow, and we get as close to the fire as we can. It doesn't take your steak long to get cold with the Alaskan wind claiming it faster than your fork can.

"Oh well, cold meat is pretty good when you're hungry."

"I'm cold."

"Me, too."

"Can I sleep in the middle?"

"No, your mother will sleep in the middle. She's a lady. You and I will each sleep on the edges in case of trouble."

"Trouble?"

"Yeah, in case there's a bear."

"A bear?"

"Yeah, a big Alaska Brown bear. They're everywhere."

"Here? Where we are?"

"I can't see one now."

"Hide all the scraps."

"Sure. Why?"

"The bears might smell them."

"How about me? Can they smell me?"

"I guess so."

"I'm putting on perfume. I definitely don't want a bear to smell me."

"Tim, do you have a gun?"

"Yeah, a shotgun and a pistol."

"Good. A double-barrel shotgun?"

"Yeah."

"That'll hold him, I'm sure it will."

"What's that noise?"

"Momma, I know that was a bear."

"I'm getting in the tent. Not that I'm scared, John Carter, I'm cold."

"I'm cold, too. It's pitch-black dark. We can't see anything."

"I see some eyes."

"That's caribou," says Tim.

"How do you know that? There's no sign on the front of those eyes saying caribou. They don't eat you, do they?"

"I don't think so."

"We'll turn in early."

"It's not early, it's almost midnight. It'll be daylight soon."

"Soon I've got to get some rest. I've got the sore throat. John, could you get a little closer? I need to put another pair of underwear on tomorrow."

"Tomorrow, I need them tonight. Momma, I think it's zero."

"What was that?"

"That?

"Yeah, that. John, you look. You crawl out that little hole we just crawled into and see if that's a bear."

"That's probably Tim."

"I saw Tim get in his tent."

"Maybe he'll go see."

"Where's the guns?"

"He's got them."

"What if the bear is between our tent and his. He could shoot it."

"Yeah, and us at the same time. Be quiet, June. Let's go to sleep. It'll be daylight in a minute. I need more than a minute."

My back hurts. Where's the flashlight? I am definitely lying here on my down sleeping bag, on my bag of land and dirt and rocks, between my husband and son with a stocking cap pulled over my eyes. It couldn't have been more than five minutes, my back hasn't had time to stop hurting. "Where's John Carter?"

"He's gone to the toilet."

"The toilet? Where? I need one. I needed one in the night last night. I mean the three hours that we called night."

"He's behind that bush."

"That bush is not big enough for me to hide behind. I'll not go."

"June, we can't pull over once we start in the rapids."

"What rapids?"

"The rapids on the Tikchik Narrows."

"Tim, have you ever floated this river?"

"No."

"I'm glad somebody has."

"Oh yeah, he floated it."

"Who did? Who's he?"

"The guide at the lodge."

"At the lodge?"

"We sent him up to see if he could make it."

"He made it, didn't he?"

"Oh yeah, he's our best guide."

"The best?"

"Didn't see but one bear."

"Only one?"

"Yeah, in his tent. It was trying to get to his flour and coffee. After it ripped the end of his sleeping bag off. Woke him up, too."

"John, I'm not having a good time. I want to go home."

"We're going. Just get into the raft. We're on our way."

"I want to stop at the first store and telephone that little plane to pick us up."

"Up? Up off of what?"

"Maybe if it would fly low, I could grab a wheel."

"Grab your breakfast. Let's get in the raft and go. We're fishing now, for salmon."

"Yeah, and char."

"I'm secure here on the front. How far is it down this river?"

"About seventy miles, I think."

"Seventy miles? You mean, 5,280 feet, one mile at a time, fast? This water is not gentle like we floated down last night. Let's go back to the mouth of the Tikchik. There, where the plane landed in that lake. *That* is where I want to go."

"Don't drop anything overboard."

"Where's the motor?"

"What motor? We don't need a motor. It's all downhill."

"I can see that. Could I have a paddle? Sit down, John Carter. Hang on. Oh my goodness. How come we didn't turn over? It's bad enough, this turning around."

"I got one. I got one."

"A salmon. John Carter's got a salmon. String him up, Tim."

"Oh, we can't."

"What? Why?"

"Well, we only keep what we can eat. We take care of all the others and put them back."

"Put them back? These big fat fish. You're going to put them back?"

"Sure, they'll spoil."

"Maybe not by tonight—when we get back to the lodge."

"Oh, we won't make it tonight."

"What?"

"Nor tomorrow night."

"What?"

"I got one. What's this? I didn't get a salmon."

"Good, that's a char."

"I never heard of a 'char.' "

"They're wonderful."

"If they are so wonderful, why are you throwing it back?"

"Look out for the sweepers."

"What's a sweeper?"

"That's when a big tree falls over the river, and you're caught in the rapids and you can't avoid it."

"I'm definitely going to avoid it. How did the guide and all those other people avoid it?"

"He's good. He said there were a few sweepers. Just be careful. There were no others."

"No others? Sweepers?"

"No, people. He's the only one. Yes sir. He said Johnny Cash wants to take his wife and boy where no one has ever been. He always delivers. He made it, and I'll bet we make it, too."

"Are all you people up here in Alaska like this? I want some insect repellent. I want these mosquitoes off. It's too cold for them."

"They don't know it, Momma. I'm hungry."

"I've got to go to the toilet. Look for a big bush. Looks like a sandy beach to the left. Pull in there, Tim. Right there. You passed it, Tim. You just fast floated right on by."

"John Carter, if we see another place like that, I'll head her in. John, you jump out, dig your heels in the sand. Jump out, John Carter, and put your brakes on. Watch your hands, that they don't get rope burned. I'll paddle her in if I can. If I can't, run like mad and grab me, cause if we go on, we sure can't come back and get you."

"I'd just as soon not jump, Daddy."

"I don't have to go to the toilet any more."

"Watch out. There goes my new bag. I need it."

"What was in it?"

"All my toilet articles, extra clothes, my makeup, lipstick, brush, things like that."

"I always liked you without makeup, Momma."

"More bushes in the water, watch the little rift. It can't go one way, and us the other."

"I don't like this floating backwards. It's shallow here."

"John Carter, put on your waders."

"I've had 'em on all day."

"If you happen to get in water over your head, son, don't panic. That can kill you. Just call for help, and we'll save you. Me. I'll save you right away. Just don't panic."

"We're not moving now."

"Lunch. Let's eat lunch."

"There's a moose."

"There's another one."

"They look like they know us."

"They're awful big. I hope they stay over there on the other side of the river."

"I'm gonna wade here, Mom."

"Be careful, John Carter."

"He sure can cast. He puts that fly anywhere he wants it. If we could have kept all our fish, we'd have a boat full."

"And where would we be? No ice."

Oh. Fish, fish, fish. Big ones, little ones. All gone back to the Tikchik Narrows.

Good gourmet lunch by Tim and we're on our way.

"Momma, Momma."

(Quietlike.)

I see the top of his fishing hat floating with the water into the rapids. The young guide, Tim, dives past me into the water and just as the current pulls down my son, he has hold of him. The struggle wouldn't have been so hard, except that John Carter walked off a sandy bank and into water over his head. How deep, I don't know. A deadly undercurrent sucked him in, until the waders that he wore were pulled under, and the water started to fill his boots, the legs, then the body of the rubber wader. I don't know what the weight was as the Tikchik Narrows pulled my son under, but I've never seen a braver young man than Tim. Somehow, by the time John can reach them, Tim has pulled John Carter, extra water, and waders out, and he still wears his old fishing hat. He spits water—reaches for his fly rod.

He has not panicked. We build a fire, dry some clothes, and thank God. Somehow we are into a more serious day. There is no turning back. We catch a lot of fish, sing "North to Alaska" with great gusto.

Sometimes the animals come close—look us over and just walk away. We are the intruders. A gentle ride again. The serenity of hearing nothing except frogs and the rippling waters wins my heart, and I begin to feel like a pioneer woman. Who needs makeup?

Or insect repellent?

Or toothbrush?

Or Mentholatum?

Or hand lotion?

Or more coat?

I do.

Oh well, the bottom of the river claims them back aways. They are hugging dirt under the river, watching the current fly by overhead.

"More rocks now. Watch for the rocks. John, keep the little raft in line. Hang on. Backwards. Round and round. Don't let go, son. Paddle John, paddle Tim, pray June."

"Oh God. How much further is it?"

"It's a long way."

"There's a sweeper! In front—dead ahead."

A three-foot-wide tree, thirty feet straight across. Limbs in all directions. The water's too fast. We can't get around. Fast. Faster than the swirling water. Tim jumps to the right of the raft, digs his boots through rocks over and over, to the bank. He digs both feet into the muddy bank, holds on with his hands to a rope that burns as it pulls against the current. We slide to the right. John dives for the bank. We've caught, but the little raft whips around and drags Tim and John downstream. John Carter and I manage to help secure the raft and tie it to something on the right bank, and we stop just short of the deadly sweeper. John and Tim (his hands bleeding) are lying on the bank to the right, holding to the little raft that is bouncing to and fro, up and down against the sweeper. It's good to just get a deep breath.

We'll have to drag the rafts around and so we do. We rearrange the supplies. John takes a paddle and gets into the smaller raft to try to manage it alone. Tim sets out to paddle and steer for John Carter and me.

We catch char for supper. Tim broils them in lemon pepper in aluminum foil. They are wonderful. We make camp on another shallow bank and listen for wolves or sounds of life. There are none. We are in a most lonely place. We have food and shelter, but the darkness is upon us. We are very tired, and Tim's hands are raw from the rope burns. We are all in a high-stress position, as we ready ourselves for the baked feet in front of the fire and the frozen rear sticking out aways. I dry John Carter's clothes. We warm our shoes and dry our socks. Tim watches. The three-hour night passes our sleepy heads fast.

Breakfast.
Breakfast.
John talks to Tim alone. He looks tired. He is tired.
We pack and leave—on the Narrows again.

"John, when I was out looking for my big bush, I saw signs. Big signs."

"A bear. A big one."

Tim watched him all night. The bear watched Tim all night. He sat in front of our tent, shotgun in hand, knife and pistol in belt.

Float—slow—fast. End after end. We do not look back.

"How much farther is it?"

"I don't know."

"My throat is sore. I hope it doesn't rain."

More salmon, more char. More dead salmon, half-eaten now. The banks are worn down by the bedding of the bears.

"They are big bears, aren't they, Momma?"

"Yes, son."

"They won't hurt you, Momma."

"I know, son."

"How could my face be so burned with it so cold?"

Lots of rocks now. John managing small raft all right. His hands are blistered.

"Do you think we'll make it tonight?"

"We could. We just might."

"Keep trying, Tim. It can't be far."

Three hours later.

Tired, sore, hungry, and sleepy. We'll camp ahead there, where you see the rocks on that flat place.

No one complains as dark catches us. We literally dig through thousands of stones the size of plums and apples—pitch our tent—eat our baked char—no fresh vegetables now—drinks scarce—water all right. Very tired and thirsty. The Tikchik Narrows curve and crawl and balk their way through my short dreams.

John's hands are blistered. Tim's are raw. John Carter is still fishing. Breakfast is bleak.

"We must be near."

"Yeah, we must."

"Yo—yo—ahead—yo."

Silence except for the rippling water.

Six more hours. Nothing except fight to stay upright. Row and row and row.

"Are you all right, son?"

"Yeah, Momma, I'm all right. You?"

"Yes, son."

"John, could John Carter and I try to row that boat a while."

"No."

"This river doesn't branch off, does it?"

"No. It goes into the big lake near the lodge."

"Lots of jagged stobs here. Lots of rocks. Watch it."

John's face very red. Some people get heart attacks from over-exertion.

Ahead there, about three miles, it looks as if the river widens. I believe we're near the lake. It's a relief not to row now and turn and twirl all the time. But, as the water reaches the lake, we are be-calmed. Now we wish for a current. We don't seem to have any. The rafts are heavy, there is no one in sight, so Tim and John start to try and row to the main lake. Hours go by. No plane—no nothing—just two rafts, gear, and four tired people in the calm waters trying to make it to the main lake. Even if we get there, it would be at least four miles to the main camp. We are nearing night again. My mouth is dry and my head hurts.

Then we hear the far-off sound of a motorboat. Oh, they've come for us. I know they have. They must be a little scared that we haven't showed up. We see two small aluminum boats coming toward us. They are full of Eskimos, young women and men with some chil-dren.

They have come to us in urgency.

"We don't believe it," they say. We heard on the radio that Johnny Cash was floating the Tikchik Narrows with his wife and boy. We've been looking for you all day."

They take rope, attach our rafts, and very slowly we make our way across the calm lake to the main lodge. They stop—rest a while—then go on their way. Later that night, we hear on the radio that both boats were lost. No one was killed, but a motor went out and the boats went over the falls south of the lake. They all made it safely to shore some way.

This was not really considered a dangerous river to float, but, for me, it was a very serious river, a time for thankfulness that I will never forget, and a true love for the sounds you hear in the night. The clean air—Alaska makes you feel brand new, and there's nothing like a little excitement to remind you that you're still married to Johnny Cash. I have great respect for a young guide named Tim and love the way they take care of you and yours at the Tikchik Narrows Lodge. There's a real bed to sleep in, and wonderful cooks that don't run out of food.

June, John Carter, and John in Melbourne, Australia.

DOWN UNDER

We've toured pretty much all over the world. (I don't want to go to those places we haven't toured—Sri Lanka, Antarctica, or Tibet. Each place is new, exciting, and I am always so glad to get home.

I am not yours, Gordon. No thank you, thank you. Please. I've written your name on my arm like you asked me to—see—right here above the elbow. It says Gordon. Just like on your arm that says June, right? Now let go, slowly. The blood should start to flow in my arm again. No—no thanks. I don't want that nugget of gold. You may keep it. John, where are you?"

I could not see him anywhere. I could see the bodies and the kinky hair. I could see the dead skin on the people and the smiles on their faces that showed those white, white teeth and the lost look that hid behind their eyes. They were singing "I fell into a burning Ring of Fire, I went down, down, down and the flames went higher"—and I could see the fire, too. It was blazing higher and higher. They danced a kind of native dance of the far-out outback Australian aborigine. Some were drunk from a native beer that they had made themselves. I was lost in about one hundred people. Our manager, Lou Robin, was trying to save John—for these people had heard him on the radio, and they really did know who Johnny Cash was. They talked their native language, then broke into "I Walk the Line." They got as close as they could, crowded and danced around you, your friends, and the car you came in. I was being pulled or pushed, but mostly dragged by Gordon, who wanted me for his very own.

"No, Gordon. I'm not yours. I'm Johnny Cash's wife. Don't you understand. I don't like kangaroo."

Lou screamed, "Like it, June. Like anything they offer you. Just take it, eat it, and smile."

"Where's John? I need help here. I don't like this party. Help me, Lou."

"I'm trying to help myself."

I finally saw John. About eight aborigine women were having a tug of war over him. He was laughing, but the tug was heavy, and he was as tired as I was.

"Where are they cooking the kangaroo?" I screamed.

"In the fire, in the fire."

Then I saw it. The huge tail, hair, and all-standing tail on end in the burning sticks. What a barbecue. I might as well try to laugh.

They crowded in closer and closer. I was finding it hard to breathe. How did I get cut off from the others? "Help!" I cried.

"Up here," Jan screamed. She was lying belly down on top of our car, reaching for my arm.

I crawled up. Gordon was content to push. I lay face down on top of the car, and we now had a better point of view of life in the Outback.

"Here, here." Big Gordon had bounded through the crowd, pulled on the burning kangaroo's tail, retrieved a big hunk—half raw and hairy—and was smiling again, offering me this delicate prize.

I tried to remember what the Ambassador's wife had said to me. "Don't offend them. Eat what they give you. It won't kill you."

I threw it into my mouth, swallowed tail, hair, and all in one gulp. "Thanks, Gordon, that was wonderful. No, Gordon, you can't get up here on top of this car. It won't hold you. Stay down there. No, I don't want your dingo dog, either. What's this? I've got to eat this? This is definitely a worm. It's not? Good. I'll just close my eyes and swallow. Not too bad, that little morsel that looks like a white worm. Good for me, right, Gordon?"

These kind people fed us their best—their kangaroo—their witchid grubs—tried to give us their gold. They did care for us, these natives of Australia who sang their farewell to us as we drove away . . .

  While I was singing
  Somebody touched me
  While I was singing
  Somebody touched me
  It must have been the hand of the Lord.

John and John Carter.

THE AUSSIES

They'll take a four-wheel drive and climb a tree. Man, woman, or child. They can do anything. They're tough. They can muster catter, they can make a pablovia—a fruitcake. They can drink our worst drunk under the billiard table. They carry a billy for the making of the tea. They'll sleep out on the hard ground and look for the spots on the sun. They'll show you the Southern Cross and dare the world to say it isn't theirs alone, hanging in their sky. They'll show you a swagman—play you a "digger a do"—and take you "Waltzing Matilda." They'll feed you lamb that does not taste like mutton. You'll wear a sheepskin jacket, a slouch hat, and eat real good.

Did you see him? It was him, I tell you. He come down out of the mountain right here—just now. You just missed him, Mate. It was him, I tell you. Alive he was, Mum, in the truck with Doctor Potanin. No, I'm not drunk, Mum. I say, Mate you look just like Johnny Cash on the television. You know that, Mate? And he gets out of that truck, Mum, and he belts out 'I Walk the Line.' Sung it to me, right here by my ticket gate. It was him, I tell you. He was big, big, I tell you. I always thought he was smaller than that. I said, if you're really Johnny Cash, sing me 'Ring of Fire.' He lit right into it, singing it without any music. I'm not drunk, Mum. All my life I only wanted to meet him in person. I been a fan for thirty years and right here near this border of New South Wales and Victoria at Stanthorpe, he just appeared. God sent him down from the mountain, I tell you. All the way down under here from America. Hurry and get through. I'm on my way to the pub. They'll never believe me, no sir, they ain't gonna believe me."

And do you know that they didn't believe the little man from the ticket gate at the pub? The more he hollered about it, the more his friends didn't believe him, the drunker he got.

Dr. Potanin, wife Annie, John, and I pulled into the little town of Stanthorpe near the pub. An old fellow came staggering out of the pub over to the truck.

"There's this idiot in there, says he's seen Johnny Cash come down out of the mountain. He's crazy, Mate. Crazy, I tell you. Nobody believes him. I don't either. Craziest thing I ever heard of."

Dr. Potanin said, "I'd like you to meet Johnny Cash and his wife, June."

"Naw," he said. "It ain't so. It can't be so." He laughed, he tipped his hat and went waddling on down the street singing,

"I hear the train a-comin'
It's comin' round the bend
And I ain't seen the sunshine
Since I don't know when . . ."

We do visit our friends, Con and Annie Potanin, her parents, Clem and Lou, on a four-thousand-acre ranch near Stanthorpe, Australia, when we can. We also tour Australia every two years.

TWO ROSES ON THE SAME BUSH

*Like it or not our daughters are show business
too. John's Rosanne gave Reba McIntyre a
good battle for Country Music Performer of
the Year, and my Rosey, for her sins, works
the club circuit at times. She's also back in college working on her R.N. Once in a while we
get together.*

John and oldest daughter, Rosanne Cash.

No, I don't have the seven year ache. That's not me. That's my sister, I should say my stepsister, but Momma hates the word step. I'm Rosey Carter, not Rosanne Cash. She has dark hair. I have blonde hair. No, that's not her bill—Rosanne's, I mean. That's my bill. Rosanne doesn't have any bills. I'm the one with all the bills. Rosanne's the one with the big hit record 'The Seven Year Ache.' I'm going to have a big hit soon. I'm Rosey Carter; I'm the Wildwood Rose."

These are some of the things that I've heard my youngest daughter, Rosey Carter, say time and time again. It's confusing in our family. We have the Rose Bushes.

Rosanne Cash is our eldest daughter (John's by his first marriage) and mother of three—CBS records.

Rosey Carter is our fourth daughter of the six girls. She, I call the Wildwood Rose.

They used to be inseparable—these two, I mean. They had a wonderful kind of friendship that is rare and beautiful for two young women. They used to stand behind John and me on the stage and sing, slightly louder than a whisper—"Allegheny" behind our duet. They had days of being on the bus learning to play guitars and singing harmony parts. They double-dated, and John and I would sit up late to see who had gotten the "hog" this night. Their dates always seemed to constitute one Greek God and one used "hog." They would take turns getting stuck with a different "hog." Rosey married when she was seventeen, and Rosanne cried for days. Rosanne has her family now, and Rosey's not married at all. She is working hard to be a singer and is giving it all she has as the Wildwood Rose.

Our number five daughter, Cindy, and I had gone to see her.

"You want to dance, honey?"

"No. No thank you, sir. I wouldn't care to."

"How about you, black eyes? You want to dance? You sure are cute."

"No. No, sir, she doesn't want to dance, either."

"What are we going to do, Cindy? That man was a little drunk."

"I think he was big drunk, June. Maybe he knows who we are."

"No, he couldn't. it's too dark in here. It sure is a nice little club, but mercy, Rosey could have picked a place where all these men don't waltz by our table and grab us and want us to dance."

"Rosey's got a good little band."

"It sure is. I like to hear her and Roger Allen Wade sing together. Together they're great. We'll just hide here and watch their show."

"Hey, get your grubby fingers off my arm, man. Better still, get both your hands full of grubby fingers off my arm. I don't want to dance. Please, Cindy doesn't want to dance, either. We've come to watch the show. Rosey Carter and Roger Allen Wade—in Orlando, Florida—some nice little club.

"Cindy and I had left early, taken a cheap flight to Orlando. The flight had gotten cancelled around Atlanta. We'd gotten in tourist on a good commercial flight, gotten really cramped, upgraded ourselves to first class just for meanness, and had gone to give the Wildwood Rose a real boost on her little show."

"Mercy, June, here comes another one."

"This dude's got a harmonica. Hey, get your harmonica out of Cindy's ear. We're not going to dance."

"Here comes that twenty-year-old muscle-bound steeplejack with a bottle of beer in each hand again. Why don't you sit down and watch the show? Hey, Rosey, sing. 'If Wishes Were Horses' or 'It Don't Paint a Pretty Picture,' whatever you call it."

"Yeah, sing it, Rosey."

"Get off our table while you're hollering, "Sing it, Rosey." Maybe Daddy won't hear about these two men that won't go away, June. Wonder why your harmonica player doesn't find someone to dance with—he's all over the floor, dancing by himself."

"I think Roger Allen Wade is going to come down off the stage and save us, Cindy."

"Hey Mister. We're not your girls. Can't you see good in here? I'm Cindy's mom. I'm her parent. Her daddy's my husband. She is a fine girl. I am a woman with kids. Get off the table. Don't sit on it and play your harmonica. Get back out in the crowd. Cindy's husband Marty will ram you with his fiddle bow.

"Here comes that steeplejack again. He's waltzing right toward you, June, with that silly grin on his face."

"Rosey, Roger, sing. 'American by Birth' or 'Southern by the Grace of God.' Give us a good ole get down Dixie song. I follow them wherever they go—I love 'em."

"Cindy, I've got a jar of cold cream in my purse. If he grabs you again (your harmonica player, I mean) I'm hitting him with it. Hard. I'll clean him good with that jar."

"All the crowd are real nice. Look at that couple on their anniversary. He's bought her an orchid, and those young people dancing—having the best time."

"Hey, we don't need another chair at this table, especially with you in it, sir. Get your chin off the table, the chin near the mouth that still has the harmonica in it."

"Her name is not black eyes—her name is Cindy. She doesn't like you. Do you hear me?"

"Hey."

"Hey, sir. Cindy, I think your harmonica player is asleep."

"Why is he sleeping at our table?"

"Hey, Roger. Hey, Rosey. Maybe you should bring that steeplejack with you."

"Let's all get an arm and a leg and carry him outside. We should have brought Tara. She's young and pretty. She's not married. Maybe they would have liked her. Maybe she could have carried a leg here. We'll sit him up against the building."

"Cindy, I think we should just forget about our harmonica player and our muscle-bound steeplejack. I don't think Daddy and Marty would understand."

"Hey, Rosey, grab his harmonica, stick it in his mouth. It looks good with his grin. Careful, don't drop him. Roger's got an arm, I got a leg, Cindy, get an arm—muscle-bound steeplejack's got a leg."

Rosey, please try to get back on the same bush with Rosanne. Think of coliseums with air-conditioned dressing rooms instead of dark alleys behind seedy clubs. Think of limos instead of pick-up trucks. Think of a good man instead of muscle-bound steeplejacks and harmonica players. Think of your poor old mother's back.

Mother Maybelle.

MEDICARE

Mother Maybelle used to use a hot tea bag to lance a stye. We knew better; we went to a doctor. We didn't know he was a doctor who believed pain—your pain, of course—was good for the soul.

Rosanne felt lousy. One of her eyes was swollen almost shut—had shades of blue and brown hiding here and there, and on the lower lid what appeared to be a stye now took on another name. "You'll need a specialist, Rosanne. You need expert care." One eye is beautiful—dark curly eyelashes surrounding that beautiful dark brown eye that looks you straight in the eye—demands your attention, and you sit spellbound waiting to do the bidding of the wonderful good eye. It has compassion, goodness, a little meanness—this eye is definitely in control here. Almost anyone alive would follow the bidding of the left good eye.

"Rosey and I are taking you to a specialist. Keep your bad eye covered in this ice pack. Don't look out of it. It's pure blood streaked, and it just don't paint a pretty picture, Rosanne."

"I feel terrible. How can I walk one sided all day. I'll look good from my point of view where I have my good left eye."

"Rosanne, I'll try to walk close to people as we pass them. I'll turn you around where they can't see the bad eye."

"All my Vanderbilt fellow students will see my bad eye and think I've been in a terrible fight."

"Have you?"

"Of course not. One side of my face is normal. Is this going to hurt?"

"I don't think so. The doctor will be very gentle. Rosey and I will sit on each side for your moral support. This doctor is here to fix your bad eye. It's going to look just like the other one."

"Doctor, this is our daughter, Rosanne Cash. Her eye hurts."

"I can see it hurts. It's all swollen with red streaks and blue bags under the eye."

"What's wrong with it?"

"I don't know."

"You're a specialist. You've been to school."

"I want that bad eye fixed just like that beautiful eye just over her nose."

"Will it hurt, doctor?"

"No, it's not going to hurt you at all, Rosanne. Just lie down here on this table."

"I'm cold and scared."

"Rosey, get her a blanket. We're right here, Rosanne. He says it won't hurt. I think he's going to lance the stye."

"Lance? You mean with a big knife. They're going to take it and stick it in my eye to actually cut that boil. You're telling me that blade is going to be stuck in my eyeball?"

"I think that's the plan."

"Here, Mrs. Cash. Rosey, I'll need both of you to help me. You hold her. Wait. Hold her."

"Why are we going to have to hold her? Just let her lay there quietly on the table. You work your little wonder magic of putting some healing source on the eye. She'll feel better—smile—the red and the blue and black and brown eye will say good-bye to the swelling. She'll sit up—smile—we'll hug her and Rosanne will have both eyes back to the wonder that they were. Two beautiful brown eyes—do it, doctor."

"June, I'm scared. Rosey, don't let him hurt me."

By now I could see the tears in Rosey's eyes as she stood as close to Rosanne as she could get.

"Doctor, don't cause our daughter pain and discomfort. If this is serious—put her to sleep. She doesn't need to feel this pain. Just put her to sleep and you'll do your work. She'll wake up and she'll never know there was any trauma."

"These young kids have got to learn that there's pain in this life."

I looked at Rosey, she at me. We clenched our teeth and came to the full realization that we were up against a doctor who didn't believe in medication for pain. We had all been pulled into his office for an experience in growing up. "This'll toughen her up," he said.

I don't want her tough, I thought. I don't want her in shock. I just want the bad eye to go good again.

We moved nearer to the operating table (in his office). Rosey stood at Rosanne's head, and I stood at her side. We were convinced that it couldn't take long and he was highly recommended for this type of thing, but Rosey's eyes sent silent thoughts as we saw the doctor line up on a small table–pure-white-linen-cloth, one very short knife, straight to the point, ointments, tweezers, very long needle and vial, Q-tips, pads, swabs. Rosey's eyes said "why are we doing this in the office?" So far, there's only anxiety here. Nothing to stop Rosanne's pain. We should be in a big white operating room.

The doctor took a cloth with a hole in it and put it over Rosanne's head. Only the bad, sad painful eye came through with all the swelling. I know she was somewhere behind all those sheets, but she seemed to be in this room with just one bad eye that was crying.

"Doctor, can't you give her anything for the pain?"

"Who needs anything for pain. Not Rosanne," he yelled. "She's tough. She'll make it."

"I'm not tough. I don't know what's going to happen, but I don't like the way we're starting this operation."

"Hold her, Rosey. Both your hands tight against her head. She cannot move her head. I've got to stick this needle in the corner of her eye. That won't hurt either. Mrs. Cash, hold both her arms. She cannot move. This is delicate. The knife cannot slip. If she fights she could damage her eye. My nurse will hold her feet. They sometimes kick."

"Kick?"

It happened very fast. The doctor grabbed the very long needle and injected something into the corner of Rosanne's brown and blue and now red eye. If it wasn't going to hurt, why is Rosanne screaming? Why is Rosey holding Rosanne's head in both hands like a vise? Why do I have this big blue knot on my arms where Rosanne pinched me?

"Hey, Doctor. This is not the way to do this. You're hurting her."

"She's tough."

"Then why is she crying?"

"Hold still."

"I've got to open up this stye and cut out this cyst."

"What?"

"I'll make an incision here and then just behind the eyelashes. I'll just take this little instrument that looks like a spoon and spoon out the trouble."

By this time Rosey had decided to spoon out his trouble.

Give her something for pain, you fool doctor. How could you? She's crying too, now. It's all right Rosanne, but it's really not all right. Rosanne kicks with both feet as if she were searching for some faraway field goal.

"Hold her! She'll get hurt."

"It's you that's gonna get hurt!" she screamed, through her tears, as Rosey held on and washed Rosanne's face with her own tears.

"You'll have to hold her."

And we did. We pinned her poor head to the table, and this doctor that now probably has had time to read his book on compassion that I sent him—took fifteen minutes to cut the eye, remove the cyst, and sew up the eyelids. My poor Rosanne. I cried. Rosey cried and Rosanne was too far gone to cry.

We are waiting and living for the day that a certain doctor is the one behind the hole in the sheet with the blue and black and red eye. Rosey will be giving him the needle. Rosanne will have the joy of cutting, spooning, and sewing up his eyes. I'll be the one holding both his legs, ensuring him plenty of good dark green and blue marks. We will all be wearing earplugs at the time. He's tough. He can take it. But it's sad to hear a full-grown man scream and holler and cry.

June as Mayhaley Lancaster—a little, old, ugly lady.

SO MUCH FOR
MAKEUP

I'll just hunch my back up a little—screw up my face, bend over slightly—emote pain for a long last hand of applause, think death and destruction—fear for the lives of my sons, wrinkle my body from the inside to add twenty or thirty years to my life—rely on a good makeup artist, spend three hours of building wrinkles and age, age, age. Now! No one will ever know it's me. I've truly become the mother of Frank and Jesse James. The world won't know that— I hope the network won't know it either, until they see the credits. It was a challenge—Johnny Cash and Kris Kristofferson had nailed me to the wall. If you're thinking of playing Robert Duvall's mother in his preacher movie—you can surely be ours in our movie, *The Last Days of Frank and Jesse James* for NBC-TV. Nothing to it. The part is yours. "Thanks," I said. "Why can't I be the young and beautiful one some time? Why do I have to always be old, old, and ugly?"

But they had the nerve to challenge me to do it. I began to feel like their mother, Momma James. Their producer, Joe Cates, challenged me, so hurrah—here I go. No one knows it's me—right. My hair is in a knot. I'm near the grave site of son, Jesse (Kris Kristofferson), and no one knows it's me. Just walked past Frank (Johnny Cash). He didn't say Hi, Mom. I've seen two hundred people, and no one knows me—good.

Here comes daughter Kathy (John's), son-in-law Jimmy Tittle, grandson Thomas, and they're carrying their newest addition to the family, one-and-one-half-year-old Dustin. Beautiful shiny eyes—

sharp—curly brown hair—my grandson—good!! No one knows me yet. They're right up even with me. Kathy looks through me, Jimmy past me, Thomas runs on up even with me. Little Dustin has just turned his head around toward me. "Mam-ma, Mam-ma," he cries!!!

EXPO

We've traveled to country and state fairs and the Expo celebrations that seemed so popular the past few years. Mini-cities would spring up in a blighted part of town, and the people would come. Sometimes nobody told the right people.

June and Johnny at the Ford Theater in Washington, D.C.

It was Expo '84 that made me proud in Knoxville, Tennessee, one hundred miles on down into East Tennessee from our Maces Springs home in Virginia. You could see the wonderland of the fair; just at the foot of the Great Smokey Mountains, and the people came, laughed, loved, and saw a new building of many things. It must have taken millions to build all this new magic expo world of wonderlands from every country. We walked on plywood the width of the field—jumped the buckled and broken pieces that were our pathway through the giant stadium of the University of Tennessee, where the fair-goers waited in the rain, just a dewy mist, for the fireworks to go off to top off the Expo '84. We were the stars with wet feet and a happy heart that performed before the sixty-eight thousand happy hearts that took pride in putting on our show and being amazed at the massive fireworks display. They'd have never made it without that wonderful, powerful Butcher family—no, sir—them Butcher boys got this built. They got this fair put on. Someone said it couldn't be done. Ha! Look-a there. There it is. New banks, new buildings in town, too. It's them Butcher boys that did it—yes sir— Do you know them?

No, sir, but I've many friends that know them.

It was Expo '85 in New Orleans and Bob Hope's birthday. The barges lined the powerful, rough, wild Mississippi fighting its way through patrol boats and thousands of sun-parched faces and necks on both sides. It continued to twirl "gust," make tiny whirlpools, then ran on into the Gulf of Mexico. They were hoping for thirty-five thousand people that day. The old warehouses and depressed area along the river flew balloons, wore new paints, and housed the displays of the wonderful things to see. We were "Johnny Cashed" to death, fighting our way into MAX, trying to discover a new form of photography. I fought bravely to hold onto my jambalaya in one hand, while sucking the fat out of my crawfish in the other. I found out you could stick your crawfish in your mouth and still write June Carter Cash with the other, if John Carter (your son) just held you up a little with one hand as he fought off the Cajuns—yelling that Johnny Cash was a good "Coon Ass." We raced with four security guards, just trying to get through to taste some of the different foods from all the different countries. Workers sat on the sidelines admiring their work with their eyes, but praying in their hearts that all this hard work would make the New Orleans jazz heard round the world. The lines were short, and the new face of New Orleans seemed to turn from heart-warming pleasure to worrying sadness. Maybe the extra millions would come tomorrow. It's a nice fair. Sure it is. I like it. I hope the people come. We kept on hoping they would come.

Vancouver, British Columbia smiles. It just does. The clean air that enriches the flowers and shrubs and has them produce to their highest ability the prize roses, the cavalier hemlocks, the hollyhocks, and larkspur—that shine too bright for green—their color bursting forth as the morning star over the pyramid arbutus that forms the immaculate manicured hedge that seems to surround homes and city alike. In the center, along the docks, near the sailboats—the flags move. The new Expo '86 shines like the Star of India. You crane your neck as you cross the bridge on the bus to see. They are from China, Japan Russia, all the countries. They are on the grounds, they are in the streets, they are in the hotels, they are everywhere. It's clean—it shines—it glows. You hope you'll find a seat somewhere. Someone said they had seventy-five million people as of today. What did they do right?

Some street vendors line the streets selling their wares—T-shirts, drawings, and millions of earrings. Everyone buys at least two T-shirts and five pairs of earrings. Off the sidewalk you can buy sushi, chicken teriyaki on a stick—things to eat as you walk near the Expo grounds. Somehow the city itself is enough—even though the back of your mind has its intention to ride the rollercoaster—or better still, "Carlene, you ride it—it'll be good for you. John will take you if he can get through." It was riding along on this street that I saw her.

She was about five feet tall and I'm not sure she had any hair—maybe there was a little stuffed under her hat. You could see that she had made it herself or someone who sold it cheap had made it a long time ago. It was crocheted, white, and clung to her bony, tired little head showing little puffs of white hair sticking through, here and there. She wore a little white blouse, a plaid pleated skirt, and worn tennis shoes. You could see through her little plastic sack that hung over her shoulder. She carried pink and white pamphlets in the sack and also in both hands. I noticed the holes in her tennis shoes first. She was on her knees, in front of a couple just there on the street. They were patient with her—this pair. Young man about twenty, young girl about twenty. They held hands as they waited to sell their new handmade dangling earrings from India—their effort for the fair. The little old lady handed the young man her little plastic kit. It appeared to be books. They smiled at her. They were kind. She pressed a tiny white book in the girl's hand. I could only see the back side of her, but she seemed to demand their attention. They took her pamphlets, smiled, thanked her. She got up off her knees and walked on up the street. She went into an open outdoor telephone. She placed her tracts on each of the telephones as she went up the street. The traffic was heavy. We weren't moving any faster than the little old lady. Oh, my goodness, she's going right up to that skinhead. The skinhead reached, took her plastic pack of books, took the little one, and put it in the front of his leather vest.

She reached the front of the steps, about thirty of them, lined with students—one with green hair in black leather, the hair sticking up six inches into the elements. Some took the books from her and put them in their books. She weaved her way up the street, quietly but determinedly. No one turned away from her. She left her trail around the town and in Expo. You could easily follow her. I never saw anyone throw away her tracts. The streets were lined with many discarded tracts, but never hers. What is it? I said.

After checking in the hotel, I ran back down the street and took off a little packet from the public telephone.

"Are you looking for a friend?" Answer to your problems. The little white book. The scriptures gave the answers. But for some reason you could not throw it down. All through Expo I saw them—one stuck in the razor blade that was hidden in the hair of some now smiling skinhead—in the boot of a biker—sticking out of the purse of a well-to-do lady—a little boy carrying one with both hands.

This Expo is truly a success. They've already passed fifty-five million people. I hear Knoxville lost one hundred million dollars, and from Knoxville that there's real trouble in the Butcher Banking Empire. Maybe fraud and prison.

The streets near the river in New Orleans are deserted. The paint peels off the warehouses, and Vancouver grows. The shrubs shine, the flowers bloom, the fair is the fairest of the fair, and a little old lady hands out her tracts of love, peace, a way of life, and hope. I never saw her face, but I'm sure it shines, just as the faces of all she's touched. I sure wish she could have made Knoxville in '84 and New Orleans in '85.

NEW YORK, NEW YORK

New York has "bag people," homeless souls who wander the streets by day and sleep in doorways at night. And they have bottle people, who scavenge garbage cans for cans and bottles with a five-cent deposit on them. New Yorkers don't always see them. I know God does.

Cousin Joe Carter's cabin on the Holsten River in Virginia.

We ran hand in hand—pushing people, weaving in and out of the crowded streets. We were near the corner of 57th and Fifth Avenue. The windows of Bergdorf-Goodman were demanding our time. A mixture of Italian silks, tied, sewn, and stuffed made the windows come alive with a mannequin that had no breath of life or hope. People smiled—or rushed—with their heads down, walking and running all together. My friend, Jan Howard and I made a dash for the light, trying to make the other side of the street, where a newly squeezed glass of orange juice was held in the hands of the vendor hawking his wares there on that busy corner. In our rush I jumped over a bundle of newspapers in the street. As I cleared it easily— what appeared to be the finished products of the *New York Times* moved slightly and fell over. I could see the closed eyes of a human being just lying there in the mess—the feet flew by. No one stopped—all were in a hurry. "We're gonna miss the light," she cried, weaving our reluctant legs across the street. We stopped at the corner, turned around, and Jan said, "My Lord. I believe there's someone alive in there."

We stood alone in those rushing thousands that could not see the toes of their shoes that touched—kicked—and didn't seem to care that a human being was there, leaning against Bergdorf-Goodman's window of plenty. "Someone will stop," I said. "We've got to hurry," she said. But we couldn't move. The woman lay—asleep? Dead? Unconscious? In a daze? Out of it? The lost, the forgotten, was at our feet. She did not move—but she was alive. The flies crawled across her brow, which was dark brown from sun or dirt, probably a combination of both. There was gray in her hair, and she wore a stocking cap pulled to cover her hair or to give her a little warmth, as the autumn wind blew hard on the newspapers that she used as blankets—four sacks of plastic-contained stuff—some food pieces—an empty Joy perfume bottle—some clothes—a small doll (I could see through the plastic) whose hair needed combing—a brown bottle with no label—and those weird sunglasses with the turned-up edge she covered her eyes with, that closed out the world of yellow glare. A messenger raced by on his bicycle—a young model walked as if Fifth Avenue was her runway. A child ate an ice cream and held her mother's hand. "Don't look at that," the mother cried.

An indifferent dog with no leash sniffed the pile of rubble and moved on—a pigeon lit and strutted near by—a man slapped me with his briefcase. They rushed, they ran—they laughed—they sang. She lay there and did not care—or could not care.

She was breathing. "We should touch her," I said. We tried to see a pulse. The crowd pushed and shoved on by. She wore two pairs of pants and one tennis shoe—the other sticking out of one of the plastic sacks that read Carnegie Deli. . . . She had one sock on. I could not bring myself to touch her. "She's alive, Jan. I just saw her eyes blink. We've got to call someone."

"Good! Let's get out of here."

We ran back across the street, looking for a policeman, searching for a telephone. We ran into Bendel's, smelling the lovely perfume. My, that was better, wasn't it? I couldn't believe that; that was terrible.

"She was a 'bag lady', Jan. Sure was. Officer, there's a woman out there."

"Sure," he said. "Lots of them."

"This one is sick," I said. "She's lying on the street in front of Bergdorf-Goodman's front window."

"Someone *will* come along," he said. "I can't leave my post."

"We've got to use the phone."

"It's not a public telephone."

"But it's an emergency," I cried.

"Sorry, find a pay phone."

"We ran back to the corner."

"What's wrong with us? We've had first aid. We could have done something. What are we doing? Why didn't we help her?"

"I don't know."

"We've got to, you know. Let's do something *now*."

"Sure, now."

And we ran. The bags and one shoe still lay on the sidewalk, the wind blew away the pages of the *New York Times*. I picked up the page that read *The Wall Street Journal*. There was an empty hole in the debris—and an empty hole in our hearts—as the world kept whizzing by.

We turned, bowed our heads, and felt ashamed.

Oh, Lord, God, have mercy on us all—again. If you don't mind, sir, please.

PEN AND PAPER

I am a Virginia Clinch Mountain girl. I was born near the Wilderness Road. Down the "Dug Road," the "Old Reedy Creek Road," the road "Down Troublesons"—through Massican Gap. There is a part of me that clings and cries day and night for the comfort of my Clinch Mountain home in Virginia. The heart hurts in some lonesome airplane near Tokyo, Japan, and I should see Mt. Fuji, but I only can see the top of Hanging Rock through my homesick eyes. The white snow does not hug the rim of the volcano—but through the mist I see the jagged limestone that struts out over the edges and through the fog of the great Clinch. I can smell the home-cooked country ham and biscuits as I stand in the receiving line of the Ambassador's home in Prague, Czechoslovakia, waiting for my helping of the finest caviar. I should feel elated that I will see the classic cut crystal made for kings at the Moser Factory. Why do I think of the old Eye Winker pattern—pressed before the century in the home of my grandmother Addington near Copper Creek. I could stoop down and take a nugget of gold from this gold mine in Koolgarlie, Australia, put it on a chain, and wear it near the opals I've gathered today here way down yonder—and shake the red dust from my boots. Yet I hold an arrowhead in my hand, left by some long since dead Cherokee in the flat river bottom near the Holston. I smile at my friend Renata in Munich, Germany, as I try to understand her German and she my English—yet my heart yearns for the Southern dialect of an old girlfriend named Genevieve Fugate whom I haven't seen since we were soul mates in younger years—walking to church and talking about boyfriends. I love my home of glass, stone, and logs that sits on hundreds of acres in the cliff of the Cumberland River. I can hear the country music of today, but the longing of hearts in the night can remember a moon hanging over the knob—peeping through the hemlocks to the porch of our old Clinch Mountain home where I swung silently to the croaking of the frogs. I was proud on the stage at Carnegie Hall or Royal Albert Hall in London as we bowed to their cheers. Why could I not see their faces through the spotlights—only the face of my Aunt Florida shining through, saying "You were really good, honey, singing on the porch today"? I've ordered capon at the Ritz in Paris. The chef has worked his magic way, and they are bringing it now. What a sight. Why do I only see my very first capon in my valley chicken yard that I've caponized by my own hands. I called him ole ugly. I get a lump in my throat looking at the French chef's capon—tender, brown, young, and succulent. I cannot eat it. I smile as I daydream about ole ugly and how he weighed seventeen pounds when he finally died of old age.

All the world and all the places I have been, I've seen them hurt and seen sunshine faces, and yet I always stop and think of home. I wonder if that's a sin. I really couldn't care less if it is. I'll write it down with paper and pen. I may not pass this way again.